JAMESTOWN'S
Signature
READING

F

JAMESTOWN PUBLISHERS

a division of NTC/CONTEMPORARY PUBLISHING GROUP
Lincolnwood, Illinois USA

Reviewers

Vee Doverspike
Reading Chairperson
Dales Junior High School
Anaheim, CA

Sheila Kelly
Beaumont School
Portland, OR

Karen Lakin
Raa Middle School
Tallahassee, FL

Marsha Miller
Reading Specialist
Elgin High School
Elgin, IL

Lynda Pearson
Administrative Specialist, Secondary Reading
Curriculum and Professional Development
Clark County Schools
Las Vegas, NV

Lorraine A. Plasse, Ph.D.
Director of English Language Arts
Springfield Public Schools
Springfield, MA

Jane Richter
Edgewood Middle School
Mounds View, MN

Editorial Development: Juliette Underwood Looye
Interior Design: Think Design

ISBN: 0–8092–0430–4 (Pupil's Edition)
ISBN: 0–8092–0398–7 (Annotated Teacher's Edition)

Published by Jamestown Publishers,
a division of NTC/Contemporary Publishing Group, Inc.
4255 West Touhy Avenue
Lincolnwood (Chicago), Illinois 60646–1975, U.S.A.

00 01 02 03 04 05 06 07 08 09 VL 0 9 8 7 6 5 4 3 2

Contents

How to Use This Book

Working Through the Lessons

The following descriptions will help you work your way through the lessons in this book.

Building Background will help you get ready to read. In this section you might begin a chart, discuss a question, or learn more about the topic of the selection.

Vocabulary Builder will help you start thinking about—and using—the selection vocabulary. You might draw a diagram and label it with vocabulary words, make a word map, match vocabulary words to their synonyms or antonyms, or use the words to predict what might happen in the selection.

Strategy Builder will introduce you to the strategy that you will use to read the selection. First you will read a definition of the strategy. Then you will see an example of how to use it. Often, you will be given ways to better organize or visualize what you will be reading.

Strategy Break will appear within the reading selection. It will show you how to apply the strategy you just learned to the first part of the selection.

Strategy Follow-up will ask you to apply the same strategy to the second part of the selection. Most of the time, you will work on your own to complete this section. Sometimes, however, you might work with a partner or a group of classmates.

Personal Checklist questions will ask you to rate how well you did in the lesson. When you finish totaling your score, you will enter it on the graphs on page 205.

Vocabulary Check will follow up on the work you did in the Vocabulary Builder. After you total your score, you will enter it on page 205.

Strategy Check will follow up on the strategy work that you did in the lesson. After you total your score, you will enter it on page 205.

Comprehension Check will check your understanding of the selection. After you total your score, you will enter it on page 205.

Extending will give ideas for activities that are related to the selection. Some activities will help you learn more about the topic of the selection. Others might ask you to respond to it by dramatizing, writing, or drawing something.

Resources such as books, recordings, videos, and Web sites will help you complete the Extending activities.

Graphing Your Progress

The information and graphs on pages 204–205 will help you track your progress as you work through this book. **Graph 1** will help you record your scores for the Personal Checklist and the Vocabulary, Strategy, and Comprehension Checks. **Graph 2** will help you track your overall progress across the book. You'll be able to see your areas of strength, as well as any areas that could use improvement. You and your teacher can discuss ways to work on those areas.

clean

dirtiest

down

dulling

dusty

gleamed

muddiest

shining

sparkled

speck

spot

up

Antonym Pairs

1. _____

2. _____

3. _____

Synonym Pairs

1. _____

2. _____

3. _____

LESSON 1

Shoeshine Whittaker

Building Background

What did the dust say during a rainstorm?
"If this keeps up, my name will be mud!"

What do you call a jackrabbit that's stuck in mud?
"Unhoppy."

Did you smile or laugh (or groan) as you read any of these jokes? The creators of the jokes had a purpose for writing them: to entertain you. What other things have your read or seen lately that were meant to be entertaining?

Authors write for one or more of these purposes: to **entertain** (make you laugh or smile), to **inform** (explain or describe something), to **persuade** (try to get you to agree with their opinion), to **express** (share their feelings or ideas about something). Skim the story you are about to read. For what purpose or purposes do you predict Helen Ketteman wrote "Shoeshine Whittaker"?

Vocabulary Builder

1. Study the vocabulary words in the margin. Each word is half of a pair of **antonyms** (words with opposite meanings) or **synonyms** (words with similar meanings).

2. Write the antonym pairs on the first clipboard. Write the synonym pairs on the second clipboard. (Hint: Look at the word endings for a little help.)

3. As you read "Shoeshine Whittaker," underline any other antonym or synonym pairs that you find.

4. Save your work. You will use it again in the Vocabulary Check.

Strategy Builder

Identifying Problems and Solutions

- In some stories, the main character or characters have a **problem**. Throughout the story, they try to solve it. Sometimes they try more than one **solution**. By the end of the story, they usually come up with the solution that works—the **end result**.

- As you read the following paragraph, notice Billy's problem and what he does to solve it.

> Billy the Kidd thought he was in goat heaven. He lived next to Burger Doodle's favorite dumping ground. He loved nosing around in the bags of trash, looking for things to eat. Life was good—until the day the Burger Doodle became the Dino Dry Cleaners!
>
> Now where would he find good things to eat? First he tried the bookstore, but all they had were books and cardboard boxes. They were filling but not very tasty. Next he tried the pizza place, but the owners chased him away. Finally, he decided to wait outside the ice cream shop. Bingo! Before he knew it, there was an ice cream cone standing upside down on the ground like the tower of a candy castle.

- If you wanted to show Billy's problem and solutions, you could putthem on a **problem-solution frame**. It would look like this:

What is the problem?
The Burger Doodle has become the Dino Dry Cleaners.

Why is it a problem?
Now Billy the Kidd doesn't know where to find good things to eat.

Solutions	Results
1. He tries the bookstore.	1. All they have are books and cardboard boxes— filling but not very tasty.
2. He tries the pizza place.	2. The owners chase him away.
3. He waits outside the ice cream shop.	3. END RESULT: He finds an upside down ice cream cone to eat.

Shoeshine Whittaker

by Helen Ketteman

As you read the first part of this story, apply the strategies you just learned. Look for the problem that Shoeshine Whittaker faces—and why.

Mudville, which sat on the bank of the Mud River, was the **muddiest**, cruddiest town in the West. There wasn't a nook or a cranny in Mudville that wasn't covered with dirt.

One **dusty** summer morning, a stranger drove his wagon into town. The long tails of his black coat flapped as he bounced over the rutted road. He wore a bright red vest with shiny buttons that **sparkled** in the sun, and a tall top hat tilted over one eye.

"Whoa there, Miss Clara," he said, pulling to a stop at Fanny Ambrose's Saloon and Fine Eating Establishment. As he climbed **down** from his wagon, Sheriff Blackstone strode **up**. "Who might you be, stranger, and what's your business in Mudville?"

The stranger swept off his top hat and bowed. "Shoeshine's the name, and shoeshine's the game, and I figure I've found the best whang-dang town anywhere. For **shining** shoes, that is."

Sheriff Blackstone narrowed his eyes. "What in thunderation are you talking about?"

Shoeshine laughed and took a stool off his wagon. "I'll give you a free demonstration. Have a seat."

A crowd gathered as the sheriff put up his feet. Shoeshine whistled. The sheriff had the **dirtiest** boots he'd ever seen.

Shoeshine opened a wooden box filled with tins, brushes, and rags. "This is going to be one whing-ding of a challenge," he said, rolling up his sleeves. He brushed clumps of mud off the sheriff's boots. Then he opened a tin of polish and rubbed and scrubbed. Finally, he stood back. "Now that, Sheriff, is a shoeshine!"

The crowd gasped. Sheriff Blackstone blinked. "Why, my boots are as shiny as a mirror. If that don't beat all!"

Shoeshine set out a sign that read:
FINEST SHOESHINE IN THE WEST
GUARANTEED
ONLY 5 CENTS

Soon the whole town was lined up for shoeshines. By the end of the day, everyone in Mudville had beautiful, shiny shoes.

Shoeshine Whittaker counted his money. "Four whole dollars and fifty cents, Miss Clara. We have struck it rich. Tomorrow we'll head for the next town." He thanked the people and rode out of town to set up camp for the night.

Early the next morning, the sheriff shook Shoeshine awake.

"What is it?" asked Shoeshine, rubbing his eyes.

"You're under arrest for cheating the folks of Mudville, that's what! There ain't a shiny boot left in town, and your sign said 'guaranteed.'"

"But, Sheriff, I can't guarantee—"

"Shoeshine Whittaker, your sign said 'guaranteed.' Unless you can back that guarantee, you'll have to stand trial."

 Stop here for the Strategy Break.

Strategy Break

If you were to create a problem-solution frame for this story so far, your frame might look like this:

What is the problem?
Shoeshine Whittaker's sign said "guaranteed."

Why is it a problem?
There's not a shiny boot left in Mudville. Unless Shoeshine can back his guarantee, Sheriff Blackstone will arrest him.

Solutions **Results**

As you read the rest of this story, pay attention to how Shoeshine solves his problem. Keep track of his solutions, the results, and the end result. When you finish the story, you will complete the problem-solution frame.

Go on reading to see what happens.

Shoeshine gulped. "I'm the best in the West, so there's only one thing to do. Take me back to town, Sheriff. And get me rags—a mountain of rags."

Soon the townspeople had brought Shoeshine a huge pile of rags. He rolled up his sleeves. "Stand back," he shouted as he started working.

He rubbed and scrubbed and shined and polished. By noon, Mudville City Jail and Stable sparkled in the sun, and Hayden Clopstop's General Dry Goods Store and Dentist's Office shone a bright cornflower blue. Even Hayden Clopstop was surprised.

"I plumb forgot I had painted it blue," he said.

Shoeshine polished and rubbed all afternoon. By sunset, half the houses and the wooden sidewalks **gleamed**. Shoeshine worked all night long, too.

By morning, even the surface of Main Street was glistening. There wasn't a **speck** of dust or a **spot** of loose dirt in the whole town. The townspeople couldn't believe their eyes. Mudville had never looked like this.

Once again, Shoeshine set up his stool. "Now your shoes will stay **clean**. Shoeshine Whittaker guarantees it."

People lined up to have their shoes shined. By noon, the sun was high in the sky and reflecting off the shiny surfaces of the street, sidewalks, buildings, and shoes. The glare half blinded the people of Mudville. Their eyes hurt, and their heads ached.

"Now things are too shiny," complained Sheriff Blackstone.

Shoeshine pulled his hat over his ears and muttered under his breath. "These folks of Mudville are whing-dang-dingy! There's only one thing to do."

"Give me an hour, Sheriff," said Shoeshine. "I know just what you need."

Shoeshine hurried down to the Mud River. He dug mud out of the riverbank, tying it into small bags. When he returned, he set up a new sign that read:

SHINE DULLER

ONLY 25 CENTS A BAG

The townspeople lined up with their quarters. "You just take a rag and rub a bit of duller on any surface that's too shiny," announced Shoeshine. "Works great!"

The people bought every last bag Shoeshine had, and they spent the rest of the day **dulling** things up. By sunset, Mudville was back to normal.

Everyone waved to Shoeshine as he rode out of town. "You come back and visit us again, Shoeshine Whittaker," yelled Sheriff Blackstone.

Shoeshine listened to the clink of coins as Miss Clara pulled the wagon down the road. "I probably will, Sheriff," said Shoeshine, waving his top hat. "I probably will." ●

Strategy Follow-up

Now complete the following problem-solution frame with information from the second part of the story.

What is the problem?
Shoeshine Whittaker's sign said "guaranteed."

Why is it a problem?
There's not a shiny boot left in Mudville. Unless Shoeshine can back his guarantee, Sheriff Blackstone will arrest him.

Solutions

Results

✓Personal Checklist

Read each question and put a check (✓) in the correct box.

1. How well do you understand why the sheriff makes Shoeshine Whittaker return to Mudville?
    ☐ 3 (extremely well)
    ☐ 2 (fairly well)
    ☐ 1 (not well)

2. How well were you able to list synonym and antonym pairs in the Vocabulary Builder?
    ☐ 3 (extremely well)
    ☐ 2 (fairly well)
    ☐ 1 (not well)

3. How well were you able to use the information in Building Background to predict the author's purpose for writing this story?
    ☐ 3 (extremely well)
    ☐ 2 (fairly well)
    ☐ 1 (not well)

4. How well were you able to complete the problem-solution frame in the Strategy Follow-up?
    ☐ 3 (extremely well)
    ☐ 2 (fairly well)
    ☐ 1 (not well)

5. How well do you understand why the people of Mudville are happy at the end of this story?
    ☐ 3 (extremely well)
    ☐ 2 (fairly well)
    ☐ 1 (not well)

Vocabulary Check

Look back at the work you did in the Vocabulary Builder. Then answer each question by circling the correct letter.

1. Which vocabulary word is a synonym for the word *speck*?
    a. dusty
    b. spot
    c. clean

2. Which synonym pair describes Mudville when Shoeshine Whittaker arrives?
    a. dirtiest/muddiest
    b. speck/spot
    c. gleamed/sparkled

3. Which antonym pair can be used to describe directions?
    a. clean/dusty
    b. down/up
    c. dulling/shining

4. Which word from the story is a synonym of *gleamed* and *sparkled*?
    a. brushed
    b. covered
    c. shone

5. After Shoeshine sells all of his mud, the townspeople spend the rest of the day dulling things up. Which vocabulary word is an antonym of *dulling*?
    a. dusty
    b. dirtiest
    c. shining

Add the numbers that you just checked to get your total score. (For example, if you checked 3, 2, 3, 2, and 1, your total score would be 11.) Fill in your score here. Then turn to page 205 and transfer your score onto Graph 1.

Check your answers with your teacher. Give yourself 1 point for each correct answer, and fill in your Vocabulary score here. Then turn to page 205 and transfer your score onto Graph 1.

Strategy Check

Review the problem-solution frame that you completed in the Strategy Follow-up. Then answer these questions:

1. Shoeshine rubs and scrubs everything until Mudville is glistening. What is the result?
   a. Shoeshine digs mud out of the riverbank.
   b. The sheriff threatens to arrest Shoeshine.
   c. The people complain that everything is too shiny.

2. Why does Shoeshine rub and scrub until everything in Mudville is glistening?
   a. because the sheriff has threatened to arrest him
   b. because everyone wants a muddy, cruddy town
   c. because everyone wants a town to match their shoes

3. What is the end result of Shoeshine's problem?
   a. Shoeshine rubs and scrubs everything until Mudville is glistening.
   b. The people dull things up, and Mudville gets back to normal.
   c. Shoeshine gets arrested for not backing his guarantee.

4. Why is the end result humorous?
   a. because Mudville ends up muddy and cruddy, just the way it started
   b. because Mudville ends up gleaming and glistening, just the way it started
   c. because Mudville starts out gleaming but ends up muddy and cruddy

5. Aside from the fact that Shoeshine doesn't go to jail, what else makes him happy with the end result?
   a. He gets to make Mudville a clean place again.
   b. He gets to shine the shoes of everyone in Mudville.
   c. He gets to sell mud that people could have gotten for free.

Comprehension Check

Review the story if necessary. Then answer these questions:

1. Why is Shoeshine Whittaker happy when he first rides into Mudville?
   a. He knows that lots of people will need their shoes shined.
   b. He knows that no one there will need their shoes shined.
   c. He knows that he can sell the people lots of mud.

2. What does Shoeshine probably mean by "guaranteed"?
   a. He guarantees that everyone's shoes will stay shiny forever.
   b. He guarantees that he gives the best shoeshine in the West.
   c. Neither of the above answers is correct.

3. Why does Shoeshine mutter, "These folks of Mudville are whing-dang-dingy"?
   a. He wishes they'd make up their minds about what they want.
   b. He can't believe they don't know what color their buildings are.
   c. He can't believe they like their town so clean.

4. Why do the people buy mud from Shoeshine?
   a. They are used to buying things from traveling salesmen.
   b. He tells them the mud is shine duller, and it will solve their problem.
   c. Shoeshine sells shine duller cheaper than anyone else around.

5. When do you think Shoeshine will most likely visit Mudville again?
   a. When he wants to spend a night in jail.
   b. When he needs more mud to sell.
   c. When he runs out of money and needs more.

Check your answers with your teacher. Give yourself 1 point for each correct answer, and fill in your Strategy score here. Then turn to page 205 and transfer your score onto Graph 1.

Personal		
Vocabulary		
►Strategy		
Comprehension		
TOTAL SCORE	✓	T

Check your answers with your teacher. Give yourself 1 point for each correct answer, and fill in your Comprehension score here. Then turn to page 205 and transfer your score onto Graph 1.

Personal		
Vocabulary		
Strategy		
►Comprehension		
TOTAL SCORE	✓	T

Extending

Choose one or both of these activities:

PLAN SHOESHINE'S RETURN

Shoeshine Whittaker says he'll probably return to Mudville. With a partner, brainstorm something that he might try to sell during his next visit. Then use a problem-solution frame to plan a story about Shoeshine's visit. If you can, perform your story for the class.

LEARN ABOUT THE OLD WEST

Use some of the reference books listed on this page to learn more about the Old West. Choose a real town or person, and write a brief report. Or choose a legendary fictional hero, and report on what makes him or her so popular.

Resources

Books

Boomtowns of the West by Bobbie D. Kalman. Copyright © 1999 by Crabtree Publishers.

Buffalo Bill Cody: Showman of the Wild West by William R. Sanford. Copyright © 1996 by Enslow Publishers, Inc.

Complete Idiot's Guide to the Old West by Goodstat. Copyright © 1998 by Macmillan Publishing Company.

Life on the Trail by Bobbie D. Kalman. Copyright © 1998 by Crabtree Publishers.

Wagons West by Robert Shellenberger. Copyright © 1996 by Heritage West Books.

LESSON 2
The Big Toe Contest

Building Background

Suppose you heard your grandpa say, "Hey, where's the fire?" Would you understand what he meant? Well, if he saw a fire truck racing down the street, he would have meant one thing. But if he saw your little brother rushing happily toward his bike, he would have meant something else.

To understand what your grandpa meant, you would need to use context clues. **Context** is the information surrounding a word or situation that helps you understand it. When you don't have enough context about a word or a situation, misunderstandings often happen. Misunderstandings also happen when information is taken *out* of context. The following exercise will help you understand how context works.

1. Write this sentence at the top of a sheet of paper:
   ### Felix was in a real jam!
2. Think of one meaning for the sentence. On the top half of the paper, write or draw the context that would help someone understand your meaning.
3. Then think of another meaning for the sentence.
4. On the bottom half of the paper, write or draw the context that would help someone understand that meaning.
5. Explain why someone might misunderstand the sentence if the context was not clear.

Vocabulary Builder

fair

toe

1. Before you begin reading "The Big Toe Contest," use the clipboards or a separate sheet of paper to list all the meanings of *fair* and *toe* that you know. (Use a dictionary or thesaurus if you need help.)

2. Then, as you read the story, decide which of the meanings that you wrote on the clipboards are used in the story. Put a star (★) next to those meanings.

3. Save your work. You will use it again in the Vocabulary Check.

Strategy Builder

Making Predictions While Reading a Story

- When you read, you often make predictions. As you know, a **prediction** is a kind of guess that you make based on information or clues that the author provides. Those clues are often context clues. They help you understand what's happening. They also help you predict what might happen next.

- As you read "The Big Toe Contest," you will pause twice to make predictions. At Strategy Break #1, you will write down your predictions. You also will write which context clues helped you make your predictions.

- At Strategy Break #2, you will check your earlier predictions. Then you will make more predictions, and you will tell which clues helped you make them.

- After you finish reading the story, you will see if any of your predictions matched what happened in the story.

The Big Toe Contest

by James Russell

The story you are about to read shows why knowing the right context is important—and how misunderstandings can happen without it.

Hayden Tucker is my best friend, but he gets weird ideas. Like the time my grandpa and grandma took Hayden and me to the county **fair**.

I reached Hayden's house at around seven in the morning and banged on his bedroom door.

"Time to go, sleepyhead," I shouted. "The Gramps-mobile will be here any minute.

Not hearing anything, I opened the door and went in. My friend was sitting on the bed, counting.

" . . . forty-five, forty-six—"

"What are you doing?"

Hayden glanced at me. "Shhh. Don't mess me up, Rick. Forty-eight, forty-nine . . ."

I walked around the bed and stopped short. His right pants leg was rolled up to the knee, and on the end of his big **toe** was a plastic weight from his dad's weightlifting set. Every second or so, Hayden flexed his toe up, then down.

"Get your toe stuck?"

"No," he grunted. "I'm training for an important event."

I laughed. "What event? The Mr. Toeriffic Competition?"

Hayden sighed and stopped counting. He pulled a piece of paper out of his pocket and waved it at me.

"I am preparing for the River County Fair's Big Toe Contest," he announced.

I snatched the paper in mid-wave. Sure enough, in big blue letters it said:

The Big Toe Contest
$50 First Prize

"Nobody's going to give away money for people's toes," I argued.

"They will too. Says so right there. 'Prize money offered by the River County Fair.' "

 Stop here for Strategy Break #1.

Strategy Break #1

Use the information in the story to help you answer these questions:

1. What do you predict will happen next?

_____

_____

2. Why do you think so?

_____

_____

3. What clues from the story helped you make your prediction(s)?

_____

_____

 Go on reading to see what happens.

He was right. It even had an official-looking logo. "But, Hay, there must be thousands of great toes in River County. How are you going to win?"

"I've been practicing twenty minutes every day, and soaking my toe in orange juice. Vitamin C keeps you healthy."

Hayden and I inspected his big toe. It did look healthy.

Outside, a horn blasted twice. Hayden grabbed his gym bag, and we raced downstairs. The Gramps-mobile sat in the driveway. Grandma and Grandpa grinned and waved at us from the RV's high front seat.

"You boys make yourselves comfortable," said Grandma as we scrambled in. "We'll be there in an hour or so." The inside of the Gramps-mobile was fixed up like a little house, with a kitchen, a living room, and a bedroom. Grandma handed us two glasses of apple juice and a plate of warm blueberry muffins.

For the next few minutes we munched on muffins and stared out the window at the farmland. Then Hayden pulled a bottle from his gym bag. He unscrewed the cap and gave me a sniff. Phew! It smelled like gasoline and flowers mixed together.

"What *is* that?"

Hayden rubbed the liquid on his big toe. "It's supposed to keep your joints from getting stiff. I figure judges like toes that are kind of springy." Finished, he pulled two socks over his foot.

By the time we reached the fairgrounds and Grandpa had bought tickets, Hayden was so excited he was jumping up and down.

"Hold on there," said Grandpa. "Where's the fire?"

"I've got to sign up for the Big Toe Contest," Hayden explained.

Grandma smiled. "Goodness, Hayden, I didn't know you had a big toe. Are you sure yours is ready to be judged?"

Hayden patted his bag. "Of course it is. I've been taking care of it for a whole month."

The other Big Toe contestants were a lot older than Hayden, but he wasn't worried. "I bet *they* haven't been lifting weights," he whispered, climbing onto the stage. He stood between a man wearing overalls and a woman in a red-flowered dress. All the contestants were carrying small bags or boxes.

Two men with badges clipped to their pockets walked onstage.

"We'll get started in a minute," one said, "but first we'd like to say a very special hello to our youngest contestant, eleven-year-old Hayden Tucker."

Hayden grinned as the crowd applauded.

Then the judges announced, "Contestants, display your big toes," and craziness hit the stage like a thunderstorm as people dug into their boxes and bags. I lost sight of Hayden. Then I heard Grandma gasp. A little girl next to me giggled.

 Stop here for Strategy Break #2.

Strategy Break #2

Use the information in the story to help you answer these questions:

1. Do your earlier predictions match what happened? _____ Why or why not?

_____

_____

2. What do you predict will happen next?

_____

_____

3. Why do you think so?

_____

_____

4. What clues from the story helped you make your prediction(s)?

_____

_____

 Go on reading to see what happens.

"Mommy, look-it that boy!" she squealed.

I looked. Hayden was sitting on the stage with his right foot stuck high in the air, his naked big toe wiggling like mad. The other contestants still had their shoes on. Each of them was holding up a small pickle. It was a West India gherkin, Grandma told me later. Folks around here called them "big toe" pickles because they grew short and stubby, just like a lot of people's big toes.

At that moment everybody was busy laughing—except Hayden. First his face turned red, then green.

But all of a sudden he must have decided the whole thing was pretty funny because he started grinning. Then he wiggled his toe again. The crowd laughed louder.

Eventually, the judges stopped laughing and started judging. Hayden didn't win the fifty dollars, but he did get a ribbon for having the funniest big toe in River County.

On the trip home, I couldn't resist teasing him.

"Boy, *toe*day was *toe*rrible," I said. "Hope it wasn't *toe* hard on you."

Hayden just grinned. "Wait until next month," he said. "My aunt's dance troupe is looking for toe dancers. I can't wait to try out."

I groaned. Hayden Tucker's big toe in a tutu? It was *toe* horrible to think about! ●

Strategy Follow-up

Go back and look at the predictions that you wrote in this lesson. Do any of them match what actually happened in this story? Why or why not?

_____

_____

_____

_____

_____

_____

_____

_____

_____

_____

_____

_____

_____

_____

✓Personal Checklist

Read each question and put a check (✓) in the correct box.

1. How well do you understand what happened in "The Big Toe Contest"?
   - ☐ 3 (extremely well)
   - ☐ 2 (fairly well)
   - ☐ 1 (not well)

2. How well were you able to use the information in Building Background to figure out the misunderstanding in this story?
   - ☐ 3 (extremely well)
   - ☐ 2 (fairly well)
   - ☐ 1 (not well)

3. How well were you able to use the definitions of *toe* to figure out the misunderstanding in this story?
   - ☐ 3 (extremely well)
   - ☐ 2 (fairly well)
   - ☐ 1 (not well)

4. How well were you able to predict what would happen next in this story?
   - ☐ 3 (extremely well)
   - ☐ 2 (fairly well)
   - ☐ 1 (not well)

5. How well were you able to understand why Hayden won the "funniest big toe" award?
   - ☐ 3 (extremely well)
   - ☐ 2 (fairly well)
   - ☐ 1 (not well)

Vocabulary Check

Look back at the work you did in the Vocabulary Builder. Then answer each question by circling the correct letter.

1. What does Hayden think when he reads "The Big Toe Contest, $50 First Prize"?
   a. He thinks he can win $50 for having the best big toe.
   b. He thinks he can win $50 for having the best gherkin pickle.
   c. He thinks he'll have to pay $50 to win first prize.

2. Which meaning of *toe* fits the context of the contest?
   a. part of the foot
   b. West India gherkin pickle
   c. dance performed on the toes

3. Which sentence reveals the true meaning of *toe* in the Big Toe Contest?
   a. On the end of his big toe was a plastic weight.
   b. Folks around here called them "big toe" pickles.
   c. Hayden Tucker's big toe in a tutu?

4. Which meaning of *fair* fits the context of this story?
   a. passable
   b. not cloudy or stormy
   c. place with rides and contests

5. What other meaning of *fair* could be used to describe the outcome of the Big Toe Contest?
   a. according to the rules
   b. having light hair and skin
   c. place where crafts and other items are sold

Add the numbers that you just checked to get your Personal Checklist score. Fill in your score here. Then turn to page 205 and transfer your score onto Graph 1.

Personal	
Vocabulary	
Strategy	
Comprehension	
TOTAL SCORE	✓ T

Check your answers with your teacher. Give yourself 1 point for each correct answer, and fill in your Vocabulary score here. Then turn to page 205 and transfer your score onto Graph 1.

Personal	
Vocabulary	
Strategy	
Comprehension	
TOTAL SCORE	✓ T

Strategy Check

Look back at what you wrote at each Strategy Break. Then answer these questions:

1. At Strategy Break #1, if you predicted that Hayden would win the contest, which clue would have best supported your prediction?

   a. Hayden is exercising his big toe when his friend Rick arrives.

   b. Hayden's friend says that no one will give away money for people's toes.

   c. Hayden is sitting on his bed counting when he friend Rick arrives.

2. Which meaning of *toe* does Hayden think the paper means?

   a. anything shaped like a foot

   b. part of the foot

   c. part of a stocking or shoe that covers the toes

3. If you first predicted that Hayden might win the contest, which clue might have caused you to change your prediction?

   a. Craziness hit the stage as people dug into their boxes and bags.

   b. "I bet they haven't been lifting weights."

   c. Two men with badges walked onstage.

4. Grandma gasps, and a little girl giggles. What might you have predicted caused their reactions?

   a. While others pull things out of bags or boxes, Hayden pulls off his sock.

   b. It's becoming clear that Hayden had misunderstood "Big Toe Contest."

   c. Both of the above answers are correct.

5. If Hayden tries out for his aunt's dance troupe, what do you predict he will probably do first?

   a. start exercising his big toe again

   b. find out exactly what a toe dancer is

   c. start growing a West India gherkin

Comprehension Check

Review the story if necessary. Then answer these questions:

1. At the beginning of the story, why is Hayden excited about going to the county fair?

   a. He wants to go on the amusement rides.

   b. He wants to ride in the Gramps-mobile.

   c. He wants to win The Big Toe Contest.

2. Why does Hayden say he's been soaking his toe in orange juice?

   a. He wants his toe to be healthy.

   b. He wants his toe to be flexible.

   c. He wants his toe to be strong.

3. Why is Hayden jumping up and down before the contest?

   a. He loves pickles and can't wait to eat one.

   b. He is excited about being in the contest.

   c. He is warming up his toe for the contest.

4. How are a West India gherkin and Hayden's big toe similar?

   a. They are both short and stubby.

   b. They both have their own contest.

   c. They are both green and flexible.

5. Why does the narrator use words such as *toeday*, *toeribble*, and *toeriffic*?

   a. to show Hayden that he likes his big toe

   b. to make fun of Hayden's big toe

   c. to make fun of Hayden's misunderstanding

Extending

Choose one or both of these activities:

MAKE UP A CONTEST

Work with a partner to think of a multiple-meaning word that you could use in a contest. For example, a Dressing Contest could be for the best-tasting salad dressing, the best-tasting turkey stuffing, or the best-looking outfit on a teddy bear or doll. If you'd like, you can use some of the books listed on this page for ideas. The riddle books might work especially well.

Present your contest orally without giving away the correct context. Have your classmates predict what the contest is really for. Then show a poster for the contest, with a drawing that makes your meaning clear.

EXPLORE COUNTY FAIRS

Find out about an item, an animal, or a performance that is often exhibited at a county fair. Learn what it would take to make your chosen subject a winner. Include some winning facts about your subject, such as the weight of the largest county-fair pumpkin, the speed of a barrel-jumping horse, or the markings on a grand-champion bunny. Report your findings to your class in a booklet about your subject.

Resources

Books

Do the Funky Pickle by Jerry Spinelli. Copyright © 1995 by Apple.

Funniest Riddle Book in the World by Morrie Gallant. Copyright © 1996 by Sterling Publications.

Karen's Cooking Contest by Ann M. Martin. Copyright © 1998 by Little Apple.

Kwanzaa Contest by Miriam Moore. Copyright © 1996 by Hyperion Press.

Best Riddle Book Ever by Charles Keller. Copyright © 1998 by Sterling Publications.

Magazine Articles

"Let's Go to the Fair!" *Countryside and Small Stock Journal.* May–June 1998, v82, n3, p. 71–72.

"Make Up a Joke," *Boys' Life.* October 1995, v 85, n 10, p. 67.

"Reader Riddles," *Ranger Rick.* August 1996 v.30, n8, p. 20–21.

Web Sites

www.mta.state.mi.us/kids/county fair/index.html
Enter this Michigan County Fair site to learn what makes a grand-prize blueberry. You can also learn about other crops if you click on "Crops" and then "Crop Index."

www.react.com/playnice/contests/freestuff.html
Contests and free stuff are updated frequently. Get a taste of winning—or at least competing in—a contest.

exhaustion

exiles

forced

frightened

heartless

orders

relocate

round up

stockades

LESSON 3
The Trail of Tears

Cherokees

U.S. Government

Building Background

"The Trail of Tears" describes a cruel time in United States history. During the winter of 1838–1839, the United States government forced thousands of Cherokees living in Tennessee to walk from their homeland in the Great Smoky Mountains across several states to Oklahoma. The map below shows their route.

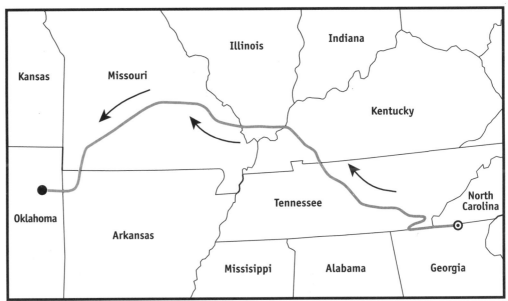

Vocabulary Builder

1. Read the words in the margin, and think about how they might relate to a forced march across many miles in wintertime.

2. On the first clipboard, write each vocabulary word that describes the Cherokees and what they experienced. On the second clipboard, write the words that describe the United States government and what it did. (Use a dictionary to find words you don't know.) If necessary, revise your choices after you finish reading the selection.

3. Save your work. You will use it again in the Vocabulary Check.

Strategy Builder

Summarizing Nonfiction

- **Nonfiction** is writing that gives facts and information about a particular subject, or **topic**.

- Sometimes when you read nonfiction, you're given a lot of information all at once. To keep the information straight—and to remember it better—it helps to stop once in a while and summarize. When you **summarize** a section of text, you list or retell in your own words just the most important ideas.

- Read the following paragraphs from an article about bamboo. Think about how you might summarize the most important ideas.

Bamboo—What a Bargain!

There are several reasons why bamboo is such a bargain. For one thing, <u>it grows fast</u>. A stalk of bamboo can grow <u>up to three feet per day</u>! So bamboo <u>can be used after only one year of growth</u>. A tree needs to grow for 20 years before it's ready to be used.

Another thing that makes bamboo a bargain is that it is <u>easy to cut</u>. A hacksaw or machete will do the job. And once cut down, bamboo is light enough that it <u>can be carried away by the work crew</u>.

Bamboo is also a bargain because it's <u>simple to use</u>. No machines, no heavy trucks, no sawmill, no steel mill—just ready-to-use bamboo.

- How would you summarize the most important ideas in the paragraphs above? Here is how one student did it:

Bamboo is a bargain because

- it grows fast—up to three feet per day.

- it can be used after only one year of growth.

- it is easy to cut.

- it can be carried away by the work crew.

- it is simple (and ready) to use.

The Trail of Tears

As you begin reading this selection, stop after each section and try to summarize the most important ideas.

A Heartbreaking Discovery

In 1828 gold was found in the Smoky Mountains. This discovery brought heartbreak to the Cherokee Nation. White men wanted the gold. To get it, they wanted the Cherokees to move away. The settlers also wanted the Cherokee land for farming. They hoped to set up their own farms with fields these Native Americans had cleared.

In 1830 the United States government stepped in—to side with the settlers! The government said that the Cherokees would have to **relocate**. They would have to move west to Oklahoma Territory and set up new farms there.

The Cherokees did not want to move away. The Smokies had always been their home. The Cherokees asked President Andrew Jackson to help them, but he said no.

U. S. Troops Arrive

In 1838 United States troops came to the Smokies. They began to **round up** the Cherokees. Only 1,000 Cherokee people got away. They hid deep in the mountains. The rest of the Cherokees were caught.

Soldiers dragged men from their fields. They pulled women and children from their homes. The troops showed no kindness to the **frightened** Cherokees. The soldiers shouted at them in English. It was a language many Cherokees did not understand.

Soldiers **forced** the Cherokees into **stockades** and split up their families. Some children wound up in camps far away from their parents. The soldiers did not care. They had **orders** to move the Cherokee people.

 Stop here for the Strategy Break.

Strategy Break

Did you stop and summarize as you read? If you did, see if your summaries match these:

A Heartbreaking Discovery

- In 1828 gold was found in the Smokies—and whites wanted it.
- To get it, they wanted the Cherokees to move.
- They also wanted Cherokee land for farming.
- In 1830 the U.S. government said the Cherokees would have to relocate to Oklahoma Territory.
- The Cherokees didn't want to move. They asked President Jackson to help them, but he said no.

U.S. Troops Arrive

- In 1838 U.S. troops began to round up the Cherokees.
- Only 1,000 Cherokees got away; the rest were caught.
- The troops showed no kindness to the frightened Cherokees. They had orders to move the Cherokees.

 Go on reading.

A Long, Hard March

When the camps were filled the long march began. Armed soldiers put the Cherokees into 17 large groups and pushed them west. About 15,000 Cherokees set out.

The march was grim from the start. The Cherokees were herded onward like cattle. Some were shoved into wagons. A few rode on horses. Most of the people had to walk. They did not have enough blankets or warm clothes. Many did not even have shoes.

Children cried as they waved good-bye to their mountain homes. Men and women also cried. As one Cherokee said during the farewell, ". . . all look[ed] sad like when friends die."

Oklahoma was a thousand miles away. To get there, the Cherokees had to tramp through mud and dust. They slogged through rain, sleet, and snow. John Burnett was a soldier on the march. He later wrote about that time. "The sufferings of the Cherokee[s] were awful," he said. "The trail of the **exiles** was a trail of death. They had to sleep in the wagons and on the grounds without fire. And I have known as many as 22 of them to die in one night. . . ."

Death on the Trail

Some people died from the cold. They shivered and shook but could not get warm. At last, their bodies ran out of heat. Others, too tired to keep going, died from **exhaustion**. Still others died from disease; they were too weak to fight off sickness.

Hunger was always a problem. The marchers only had the food they could carry with them. Their grain sacks got wet and were soon filled with bugs. No one had enough to eat. They all grew weak. Many Cherokees starved to death.

Cruel Treatment

The soldiers saw the pain and death they were causing. Yet they kept the groups of Cherokees moving anyway. It was hard for old people to keep up the pace. The **heartless** soldiers whipped them to make them move faster.

Mothers with young children struggled along. Burnett told of one woman with three small children. She set out ". . . with a baby strapped on her back and leading a child with each hand." As Burnett told it, "the task was too great for that frail mother. . . . She sank and died with her baby on her back and her other two children clinging to her hands."

There was no time to give the dead funerals or burial. The soldiers forced the groups to keep moving. Bodies of the dead were thrown into ditches dug along the trail.

After about six months, the march ended. The Cherokees had reached Oklahoma. By then 4,000 people had died. More than one fourth of those who set out died on the Trail of Tears. ●

Strategy Follow-up

On a separate sheet of paper, summarize the rest of this selection. Use your own words. Be sure to list only the most important ideas, and skip unnecessary details.

✓ Personal Checklist

Read each question and put a check (✓) in the correct box.

1. How well do you understand why the Cherokees' march was named "The Trail of Tears"?
   - ☐ 3 (extremely well)
   - ☐ 2 (fairly well)
   - ☐ 1 (not well)

1. How well were you able to use the map in Building Background to follow the Trail of Tears?
   - ☐ 3 (extremely well)
   - ☐ 2 (fairly well)
   - ☐ 1 (not well)

2. How well do you understand why the Cherokees were forced to move?
   - ☐ 3 (extremely well)
   - ☐ 2 (fairly well)
   - ☐ 1 (not well)

4. By the time you finished reading "The Trail of Tears," how many words were you able to write on the appropriate clipboards?
   - ☐ 3 (7–9 words)
   - ☐ 2 (4–6 words)
   - ☐ 1 (0–3 words)

5. How well were you able summarize the second part of this selection?
   - ☐ 3 (extremely well)
   - ☐ 2 (fairly well)
   - ☐ 1 (not well)

Vocabulary Check

Look back at the work you did in the Vocabulary Builder. Then answer each question by circling the correct letter.

1. Which vocabulary word best describes how the Cherokees felt when the soldiers arrived to round them up?
   - a. frightened
   - b. heartless
   - c. exhaustion

2. The selection says that the soldiers had their *orders* to move the Cherokee people. What does orders mean in this context?
   - a. patterns
   - b. instructions
   - c. sequences of events

3. Which phrase defines the word *stockade*?
   - a. pen built to hold prisoners or animals
   - b. roadblock built to keep people out
   - c. tent that serves as a temporary home

4. Soldier John Burnett called the Trail of Tears the "trail of the exiles." What are exiles?
   - a. people who hide high up in the mountains
   - b. people who willingly move to another place
   - c. people forced to leave their home or country

5. Which words could describe the United States government and its actions?
   - a. round up, exhaustion, frightened
   - b. heartless, orders, round up
   - c. frightened, forced, exiles

Add the numbers that you just checked to get your Personal Checklist score. Fill in your score here. Then turn to page 205 and transfer your score onto Graph 1.

Check your answers with your teacher. Give yourself 1 point for each correct answer, and fill in your Vocabulary score here. Then turn to page 205 and transfer your score onto Graph 1.

Strategy Check

Review the summaries that you wrote for the second part of this selection. Then answer these questions:

1. What is an important idea in the section called "A Long, Hard March"?

   a. Soldiers dragged men from their fields and pulled women from their homes.

   b. Soldiers put about 15,000 Cherokees into 17 groups and pushed them west.

   c. Both of the above answers are correct.

2. What is not an important idea in the section called "A Long, Hard March"?

   a. The soldiers saw the pain and death they were causing.

   b. People cried as they said good-bye to their homes.

   c. "The sufferings of the Cherokee[s] were awful."

3. Under which heading would you list the idea that many Cherokees starved to death?

   a. A Long, Hard March

   b. Death on the Trail

   c. Cruel Treatment

4. Under which heading would you list the idea that old people were whipped to make them walk faster?

   a. A Long, Hard March

   b. Death on the Trail

   c. Cruel Treatment

5. In what ways did Cherokees die on the march?

   a. cold and exhaustion

   b. disease and starvation

   c. all of the above

Comprehension Check

Review the selection if necessary. Then answer these questions:

1. Why were the Cherokees forced to move to Oklahoma?

   a. The U.S. government needed to exercise its troops.

   b. Gold was discovered in the mountains where they lived.

   c. There was dry, flat land in Oklahoma.

2. Why were U.S. troops sent in to round up the Cherokees?

   a. to force the Cherokees to leave their homes

   b. to help the Cherokees have a smooth, safe move

   c. to make sure the Cherokees could travel with their families

3. Why was moving to Oklahoma so difficult for the Cherokees?

   a. The walk was long, grim, and cruel.

   b. They had to find a new way to live.

   c. Both of the above answers are correct.

4. What happened to the bodies of people who died on the trail?

   a. They were thrown into ditches.

   b. Funeral services were held for them.

   c. They were given proper burials.

5. By the time they reached Oklahoma, how many Cherokees had died?

   a. 400

   b. 4,000

   c. 40,000

Check your answers with your teacher. Give yourself 1 point for each correct answer, and fill in your Strategy score here. Then turn to page 205 and transfer your score onto Graph 1.

	Personal	
	Vocabulary	
	Strategy	
	Comprehension	
	TOTAL SCORE	✓ T

Check your answers with your teacher. Give yourself 1 point for each correct answer, and fill in your Comprehension score here. Then turn to page 205 and transfer your score onto Graph 1.

	Personal	
	Vocabulary	
	Strategy	
	Comprehension	
	TOTAL SCORE	✓ T

Extending

Choose one or both of these activities:

MAP THE TRAIL OF TEARS

Create a three-dimensional map of the route the Cherokees followed as they walked the Trail of Tears. If you have Internet access, check the first Web site listed on this page to learn more about the Trail of Tears. Also, look up the time line on the Web site, and use it to label the Cherokees' locations at various times during the march. How might weather conditions have affected the Cherokees during those times? Attach symbols such as raindrops or snowflakes to your map to show the kinds of weather they encountered in different places.

FIND OUT WHAT HAPPENED AFTER THE MARCH

Work with a research partner to find out what happened to the Cherokees after they arrived in Oklahoma. Use the resources listed on this page or ones you find yourself. Find out such information as what kinds of homes they built, how they survived, and how life in Oklahoma compared and contrasted with life in Tennessee. Take turns with your partner, and present your findings in an oral report to the class.

Resources

Books

Becoming Buffalo Snake by Robert A. Humphrey. Copyright © 1996 by Chapel Hill Press.

The Trail of Tears by Joseph Bruchac. Copyright © 1999 by Random House Books for Young Readers.

Web Sites

rosecity.net/tears/trail
Learn all about the Trail of Tears, including when specific events occurred. Click on the time line to learn more about the path the Cherokee people took.

www.chota.com/Cherokee/
Learn all about the Cherokees, both past and present, through this site sponsored by Cherokee Publishing.

www.neosoft.com/powersource/cherokee/history.html
Read another account of the Trail of Tears. Included in this site is more information about Cherokee history and the reasons behind the march.

LESSON 4

At Last I Kill a Buffalo

Building Background

As you read the following paragraph by Chief Luther Standing Bear, try to picture the details in your mind.

Ever since I could remember my father had been teaching me the things that I should know and preparing me to be a good hunter. I had learned to make bows and to string them; and to make arrows and tip them with feathers. I knew how to ride my pony no matter how fast he would go, and I felt that I was brave and did not fear danger. All these things I had learned for just this day when Father would allow me to go with him on a buffalo hunt. It was the day for which every Sioux boy eagerly waited. To ride side by side with the best hunters of the tribe, to hear the terrible noise of the great herds as they ran, and then to help bring home the kill was the most thrilling day of any Indian boy's life.

On a separate sheet of paper, sketch pictures showing what you predict might happen to Standing Bear before, during, and after his first big buffalo hunt.

buffalo hunt

tipi

quivers

rawhide

justified

honesty

herd

fatal wound

praised

Vocabulary Builder

1. Below the pictures that you just drew, write what you think might happen on Standing Bear's first buffalo hunt. Use as many vocabulary words as you can.

2. If you do not know the meanings of some of the words, find them in the story and use context to figure them out. If that doesn't help, look up the words in a dictionary.

3. Save your work. You will use it again in the Vocabulary Check.

Strategy Builder

How to Read an Autobiographical Sketch

- An **autobiography** is the story of a real person's life, written by that person. An **autobiographical sketch** is the story of a part of a real person's life.

- Autobiographical sketches describe events in the order in which they happened. That order is called time order, or **sequence**. To make the sequence as clear as possible, writers often use **signal words**. Examples of signal words are *several days later, early the next morning,* and *in a little while.*

- An autobiographical sketch is always written in the **first-person point of view**. That means that the narrator tells his or her own story using the words *I, me, my,* and *mine.*

- As you read the following paragraph, pay attention to the sequence of events. Use the underlined signal words to help you.

My name is Marissa. I've always loved making faces in front of a camera. So it was no surprise that <u>when my favorite TV show held auditions</u> in our town, I asked my mom to take me. <u>Two days later</u>, we showed up at the studio. Was I ever nervous! We filled out forms <u>for several minutes</u>, and <u>then</u> I waited to be called. <u>After what seemed like hours</u>, they called my name. I gulped and smiled. Mom wished me luck. <u>As I stood up</u>, I found my voice and introduced myself.

- If you wanted to show the sequence of events in the paragraph above, you could use a **sequence chain** like this one:

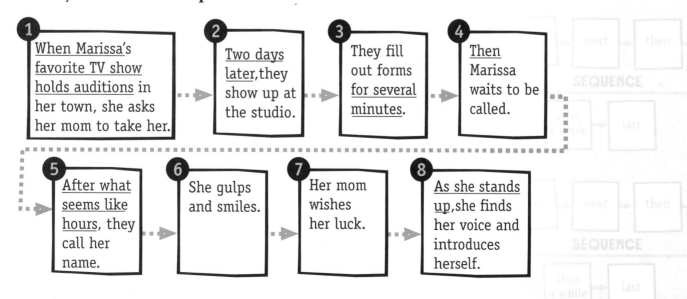

At Last I Kill a Buffalo

by Chief Luther Standing Bear

As you read the first part of this autobiographical sketch, apply the strategies that you just learned. Look for signal words as you read. They will give you a more exact picture of when things happened.

Always the evening before a **buffalo hunt** and when every one was usually in his **tipi**, an old man went around the circle of tipis calling, *"I-ni-la,"* *"I-ni-la,"* not loudly, but so every one could hear. The old man was saying, "Keep quiet," "Keep quiet." We all knew that the scouts had come in and reported buffalo near and that we must all keep the camp in stillness.

That night there would be no calling or shouting from tipi to tipi and no child would cry aloud. Even the horses and dogs obeyed the command for quiet, and all night not a horse neighed and not a dog barked.

The night preceding a buffalo hunt was always an exciting night, even though it was quiet in camp. There would be much talk in the tipis around the fires. There would be sharpening of arrows and of knives. New bow-strings would be made and **quivers** would be filled with arrows.

It was in the fall of the year and the evenings were cool as father and I sat by the fire and talked over the hunt. I was only eight years of age, and I know that father did not expect me to get a buffalo at all, but only to try perhaps for a small calf should I be able to get close enough to one. Nevertheless, I was greatly excited as I sat and watched father working in his easy, firm way.

I was wearing my buffalo-skin robe, the hair next to my body. Mother had made me a **rawhide** belt and this, wrapped around my waist, held my blanket on when I threw it off my shoulders. In the early morning I would wear it, for it would be cold. When it came time to shoot, I should not want my blanket but the belt would hold it in place.

You can picture me, I think, as I sat in the glow of the camp-fire, my little brown body bare to the waist watching, and listening intently to my father. My hair hung down my back and I wore moccasins and breech-cloth of buckskin. To my belt was fastened a rawhide holster for my knife, for when I was eight years of age we had plenty of knives. I was proud to own a knife, and this night I remember I kept it on all night. Neither did I lay aside my bow, but went to sleep with it in my hand, thinking, I suppose, to be all the nearer ready in the morning when the start was made.

We went to bed, my father hoping that tomorrow would be successful for him so that he could bring home some nice meat for the family and a hide for my mother to tan. I went to bed, but could not go to sleep at once, so filled was I with the wonderment and excitement of it all. The next day was to be a test for me. I was to prove to my father whether he was or was not **justified** in his pride in me. What would be the result of my training? Would I be brave if I faced danger and would father be proud of me? Though I did not know it that night I was to be tried for the strength of my manhood and my **honesty** in this hunt. Something happened that day which I remember above all things. It was a test of my real character and I am proud to say that I did not find myself weak.

 Stop here for the Strategy Break.

Strategy Break

If you wanted to record the main events in this selection so far, your sequence chain might look like this:

1 The evening before the buffalo hunt an old man told everyone to be quiet.

2 That night . . . all night . . . not a horse neighed and not a dog barked.

3 The night preceding the buffalo hunt, everyone got their bows and arrows ready.

4 As Standing Bear and his father sat by the fire, they talked over the hunt.

5 That night Standing Bear slept with his bow and arrow.

6 The next day Standing Bear thought about proving himself.

As you continue reading, keep paying attention to the sequence of events. Also keep looking for signal words. At the end of this selection you will use some of them to complete a sequence chain of your own.

 Go on reading.

The next morning the hunters were catching their horses about daybreak. I arose with my father and went out and caught my pony. We were joined with perhaps a hundred or more riders, some of whom carried bows and arrows and some armed with guns.

The buffalo were reported to be about five or six miles away as we should count distance now. At that time we did not measure distance in miles. One camping distance was about ten miles, and these buffalo were said to be about one half camping distance away.

My pony was a black one and a good runner. I felt very important as I rode along with the hunters and my father, the chief. I kept as close to him as I could.

The leaders went ahead until they sighted the herd of grazing buffalo. Then they stopped and waited for the rest of us to ride up. We all rode slowly toward the **herd**, which on sight of us had come together, although they had been scattered here and there over the plain. When they saw us, they all ran close together as if at the command of a leader. We continued riding slowly toward the herd until one of the leaders shouted, *"Ho-ka-he!"* which means, "Ready, Go!" At that command every man started for the herd. I had been listening, too, and the minute the hunters started, I started also.

Away I went, my little pony putting all he had into the race. It was not long before I lost sight of father, but I kept going just the same. I threw my blanket back and the chill of the autumn morning struck my body, but I did not mind. On I went. It was wonderful to race over the ground with all these horsemen about me. There was no shouting, no noise of any kind except the pounding of the horses' feet. The herd was now running and had raised a cloud of dust. I felt no fear until we had entered this cloud of dust and I could see nothing about me, only hear the sound of feet. Where was father? Where was I going? On I rode through the cloud, for I knew I must keep going.

Then all at once I realized that I was in the midst of the buffalo, their dark bodies rushing all about me and their great heads moving up and down to the sound of their hoofs beating upon the earth. Then it was that fear overcame me and I leaned close down upon my little pony's body and clutched him tightly. I can never tell you how I felt toward my pony at that moment. All thought of shooting had left my mind. I was seized by blank fear. In a moment or so, however, my senses became clearer, and I could distinguish other sounds beside the clatter of feet. I could hear a shot now and then and I could see the buffalo beginning to break up into small bunches. I could not see father nor any of my companions yet, but my fear was vanishing and I was safe. I let my pony run. The buffalo looked too large for me to tackle, anyway, so I just kept going. The buffalo became more and more scattered. Pretty soon I saw a young calf that looked about my size. I remembered now what father had told me the night before as we sat about the fire. Those instructions were important for me now to follow.

I was still back of the calf, being unable to get alongside of him. I was anxious to get a shot, yet afraid to try, as I was still very nervous. While my pony was making all speed to come alongside, I chanced a shot and to my surprise my arrow landed. My second arrow glanced along the back of the animal and sped on between the horns, making only a slight wound. My third arrow hit a spot that made the running beast slow up in his gait. I shot a fourth arrow, and though it, too, landed it was not a **fatal wound**. It seemed to me that it was taking a lot of shots, and I was not proud of my marksmanship. I was glad, however, to see the animal going slower and I knew that one more shot would make me a hunter. My horse seemed to know his own importance. His two ears stood straight forward and it was not necessary for me to urge him to get closer to the buffalo. I was soon by the side of the buffalo and one more shot brought the chase to a close. I jumped from my pony, and as I stood by my fallen game, I looked all around wishing that the world could see. But I was alone. In my determination to stay by until I had won my buffalo, I had not noticed that I was far from every one else. No admiring friends were about, and as far as I could see I was on the plain alone. The herd of buffalo had completely disappeared. And as for father, much as I wished for him, he was out of sight and I had no idea where he was.

Every one must know that I, Ota K'te, had killed a buffalo. But it looked as if no one knew where I was, so no one was coming my way. I must then take something from this animal to show that I had killed it. I took all the arrows one by one from the body. As I took them out, it occurred to me that I had used five arrows. If I had been a skillful hunter, one arrow would have been sufficient, but I had used five. Here it was that temptation came to me. Why could I not take out two of the arrows and throw them away? No one would know, and then I should be more greatly admired and **praised** as a hunter. As it was, I knew that I should be praised by father and mother, but I wanted more. And so I was tempted to lie.

I was wondering what to do when I heard my father's voice calling, *"To-ki-i-la-la-hu-wo,"* "Where are you?" I quickly jumped on my pony and rode to the top of a little hill near by. Father saw me and came to me at once. He was so pleased to see me and glad to know that I was safe. I knew that I could never lie to my father. He was too fond of me and I too proud of him.

As he came up, I said as calmly as I could, "Father, I have killed a buffalo." His smile changed to surprise and he asked me where my buffalo was.

I showed my father the arrows that I had used and just where the animal had been hit. He was very pleased and praised me over and over again. I felt more glad than ever that I had told the truth and I have never regretted it. I am more proud now that I told the truth than I am of killing the buffalo. •

Strategy Follow-up

On a large sheet of paper, create a sequence chain for the second part of this selection. Begin with event 7, and include only the most important events. Some of the chain has been filled in for you.

7 At about daybreak the next morning

8 When the buffalo saw the men

9 At the leader's command

10 It was not long before

11 All at once he realized

12 Pretty soon

13 Standing Bear shot five arrows at the buffalo calf.

14 when he heard his father calling.

15 Standing Bear showed his father where he had hit the buffalo. His father praised him

16 Standing Bear is more proud

than he is of killing the buffalo.

✓Personal Checklist

Read each question and put a check (✓) in the correct box.

1. How many vocabulary words were you able to use in your prediction about Standing Bear's first buffalo hunt?
   - ☐ 3 (7–9 words)
   - ☐ 2 (4–6 words)
   - ☐ 1 (0–3 words)

2. How well do you understand why Standing Bear was excited about the hunt?
   - ☐ 3 (extremely well)
   - ☐ 2 (fairly well)
   - ☐ 1 (not well)

3. How well do you understand why killing his own buffalo was so important to Standing Bear?
   - ☐ 3 (extremely well)
   - ☐ 2 (fairly well)
   - ☐ 1 (not well)

4. How well do you understand why Standing Bear told his father the truth about the number of arrows he used?
   - ☐ 3 (extremely well)
   - ☐ 2 (fairly well)
   - ☐ 1 (not well)

5. How well were you able to complete the sequence chain in the Strategy Follow-up?
   - ☐ 3 (extremely well)
   - ☐ 2 (fairly well)
   - ☐ 1 (not well)

Vocabulary Check

Look back at the work you did in the Vocabulary Builder. Then answer each question by circling the correct letter.

1. Which vocabulary word describes a container to carry arrows?
   - a. tipi
   - b. herd
   - c. quiver

2. Which word or phrase could have helped you predict whether Standing Bear would kill a buffalo?
   - a. buffalo hunt
   - b. fatal wound
   - c. justified

3. Standing Bear wants to prove whether his father's pride in him is justified. What does *justified* mean?
   - a. false
   - b. deserved
   - c. wrong

4. Standing Bear wears a rawhide belt around his waist. From what is rawhide made?
   - a. the skin of an animal
   - b. the teeth of an animal
   - c. the hooves of an animal

5. As he looks back on his first buffalo hunt, of what does Standing Bear say he is most proud?
   - a. his getting lost in the herd
   - b. his fatal wound to the buffalo
   - c. his honesty with his father

Add the numbers that you just checked to get your Personal Checklist score. Fill in your score here. Then turn to page 205 and transfer your score onto Graph 1.

Personal	
Vocabulary	
Strategy	
Comprehension	
TOTAL SCORE	✓ T

Check your answers with your teacher. Give yourself 1 point for each correct answer, and fill in your Vocabulary score here. Then turn to page 205 and transfer your score onto Graph 1.

Personal	
Vocabulary	
Strategy	
Comprehension	
TOTAL SCORE	✓ T

Strategy Check

Review the sequence chain that you completed in the Strategy Follow-up. Then answer these questions:

1. At what time of day did the hunters catch their horses?
   a. at about noon
   b. at about sunset
   c. at about daybreak

2. What did the buffalo do when they saw the men?
   a. they all ran close together
   b. they scattered far apart
   c. they ran straight at the men

3. Which signal words describe when every man started running for the herd?
   a. at the leader's command
   b. all at once
   c. when he heard his father calling

4. What was Standing Bear doing when he heard his father calling?
   a. shooting arrows at the buffalo calf
   b. wondering what to say about the buffalo
   c. realizing he was in the midst of the buffalo herd

5. Which signal words describe how Standing Bear's father praised him?
   a. pretty soon
   b. all at once
   c. over and over again

Comprehension Check

Review the selection if necessary. Then answer these questions:

1. What is the most important reason that Standing Bear wants to go on the buffalo hunt?
   a. He doesn't want to be left behind with all the women.
   b. He wants to get meat and hides for the family.
   c. He wants to prove that his father can be proud of him.

2. Who is Standing Bear's father?
   a. the person scouting the buffalo
   b. the chief of their group
   c. the old man who tells everyone to be quiet

3. Why is Standing Bear surprised when his first arrow hits the buffalo?
   a. He was just taking a chance with that shot.
   b. He is an extremely good shot.
   c. Neither of the above answers is correct.

4. Why does Standing Bear think about lying to his father?
   a. He thinks he should have been able to kill the buffalo with sharper arrows.
   b. He thinks he should have been able to kill the buffalo with more arrows.
   c. He thinks he should have been able to kill the buffalo with fewer arrows.

5. Based on this selection, what conclusion could you draw about Standing Bear's tribe?
   a. They work together very well.
   b. They value honesty over hunting skill.
   c. Both of the above conclusions could be drawn.

Check your answers with your teacher. Give yourself 1 point for each correct answer, and fill in your Strategy score here. Then turn to page 205 and transfer your score onto Graph 1.

Personal
Vocabulary
Strategy
Comprehension
TOTAL SCORE
✓ T

Check your answers with your teacher. Give yourself 1 point for each correct answer, and fill in your Comprehension score here. Then turn to page 205 and transfer your score onto Graph 1.

Personal
Vocabulary
Strategy
Comprehension
TOTAL SCORE
✓ T

Extending

Choose one or both of these activities:

WRITE AN AUTOBIOGRAPHICAL SKETCH

Write an autobiographical sketch about an important learning experience of your own. First use a sequence chain to order the main events. Then write your sketch. Use signal words when appropriate to help clarify the order of events. Put your finished piece together with other classmates' sketches, and bind them into a book.

LEARN ABOUT FAMOUS SIOUX

Use some of the books listed on this page to learn about an important Sioux, such as Crazy Horse, Chief Gall, or Chief Luther Standing Bear. Choose an episode in that person's life, and share it orally with the class. You might want to take notes on index cards. Then you can use the index cards as a sequence chain to help you give your report.

Resources

Books

Chief Gall: Sioux War Chief by Jane Shumate. Copyright © 1995 by Chelsea House.

Crazy Horse: Sioux War Chief by Peter Guttmacher. Copyright © 1994 by Chelsea House.

Crazy Horse: Sioux Warrior by William Reynolds Sanford. Copyright © 1994 by Enslow Publishers.

My Heart Is on the Ground: The Diary of Nannie Little Rose, a Sioux Girl by Ann Rinaldi. Copyright © 1999 by Scholastic Paperbacks.

My People, the Sioux by Luther Standing Bear. Copyright © 1975 by University of Nebraska Press.

The Sioux by Raymond Bial. Copyright © 1998 by Marshall Cavendish Corp.

Web Sites

www.littlesioux.org
View the history and present-day lives of the Lakota Sioux on the Rosebud Reservation in South Dakota. Drumming and other ceremonial music plays in the background.

www.clpgh.org/cmnh/exhibits/north-south-east-west-/lakota_main.html
Learn about the history and present-day life of the Lakota Sioux.

LESSON 5

Two Fat Boys from Venus

Building Background

How do you say hello? Do you wave? shake hands? nod your head? speak a greeting? How you say hello is often influenced by your particular culture. Your **culture** includes the customs, actions, and beliefs of the group of people you belong to. Cultures can exist among people of different age groups, geographic areas, and ethnic groups.

On another piece of paper, draw someone from a particular culture saying hello. That person may be bowing, kissing cheeks, or slapping a "high five." Share your picture with your classmates, and have them guess which culture you are showing.

abundant C

courteously c

customer D

decent a

Earth a

fainted c

gorgeous a

haircutters b

inhabitants d

screamed c

Venus a

Venusian a

Vocabulary Builder

1. Use the words in the margin to answer the questions below. Use as many words as make sense when you answer each question. You can use each word more than once.

   a. Which words might describe the setting of this story?

   b. Which words might describe the characters?

   c. Which words might describe how the characters act?

   d. Which words might describe a problem in this story?

2. When you finish reading the story, look at your answers again. Circle the words that you used accurately.

3. Save your work. You will use it again in the Vocabulary check.

44

Strategy Builder

Identifying Problems and Solutions

- "Two Fat Boys from Venus" is a science fiction story. Like fantasy stories, **science fiction** stories often contain characters, settings, or events that could not exist or happen in real life.

- Although science fiction characters can be "way out," they have **problems** just like other fictional characters do. Throughout a story, the characters will try to solve their problem. Sometimes they try more than one **solution**. But by the end of the story, they usually come up with the solution that works—the **end result**.

- As you read the following paragraphs, notice Strangely Strange's problem and the solutions he tries in order to solve it.

Strangely Strange landed his spaceship on Venus. He shined his flashlight across the surface to find what he had been sent for. Finally he saw it: a blob as big as a boulder and as sticky as a hot fudge sundae. What could it be? Strangely wasn't sure, but he had to find a way to bring a sample home to Mars.

Strangely tried rolling it, but the blob wouldn't budge. He tried zapping it, but the blob began to melt around his feet. Just before it was all melted, Strangely blasted the blob with his freezer ray. It worked! The blob froze solid. Strangely broke off a sample to take back home to Mars.

- If you wanted to show the problem and solutions, you could create a **problem-solution frame**. It might look like this:

What is the problem?
Strangely Strange has to take a sample of the blob home to Mars.

Why is it a problem?
He doesn't know how to do it.

Solutions		Results
1. Strangely tries rolling it.	→	1. The blob won't budge.
2. He tries zapping it.	→	2. It begins to melt.
3. He blasts it with his freezer ray.	→	3. END RESULT: It freezes, and he breaks off a chunk to take home.

Two Fat Boys from Venus

by Jeanne Modesitt

As you read the first part of this story, notice the two boys' problem. (It is circled.) Then notice the solutions they try, and the results of each one. (The solutions are underlined once. The results are underline twice.) Why do the boys keep trying new solutions?

One day, two fat boys from **Venus** landed on planet **Earth**. Now, these boys didn't come to Earth to take over the planet, or to scare its **inhabitants**, or to get some pointers on how to lose weight. (As a matter of fact, *all* boys from Venus are very, very fat, and it suits them just fine, thank you.)

No, the reason these two boys came to planet Earth was to get a **decent** haircut.

You see, for all its beauty and splendor and **abundant** ice-cream shops, Venus doesn't have any good **haircutters**. In fact, the last haircut the boys got was from a partially blind **Venusian** man in his mid-hundreds who fell asleep while cutting the boys' hair. Tired of one lousy haircut after another, the boys decided to come to planet Earth—a planet famous throughout the galaxy for its superb haircuts.

As they stepped out of their spacecraft, Frank, the older boy, turned to Harry.

"Where do you suppose the nearest haircutter is?" he asked.

"I don't know," said Harry. "Probably not in this cornfield. Let's go ask that farmer over there. Maybe he knows."

"Good idea," said Frank.

A moment later, they reached the farmer. "Say there," said Frank. "Could you please direct us to the nearest haircutter?"

"Someone reasonably priced, if at all possible," added Harry.

The farmer took one look at Frank and Harry and **screamed**. Then he **fainted** and fell flat on his back.

"I wonder what that was all about," said Frank.

"I don't know," said Harry. "Maybe it's the way Earth people say 'hi.'"

Just then, the farmer's wife appeared on the scene.

Frank and Harry, being polite boys, immediately greeted her in Earth fashion—a scream followed by a fall on their backs.

The farmer's wife proceeded to do the same.

Frank and Harry sat up and waited for the farmer's wife to wake up.

When she did, Frank said, "Could you please tell us where the nearest haircutter is?"

But all the farmer's wife did was scream and faint again.

 Stop here for the Strategy Break.

Strategy Break

If you were to create a problem-solution frame for this story so far, it might look like this:

What is the problem?
Two boys from Venus (Frank and Harry) have come to Earth for haircuts.

Why is it a problem?
They can't find anyone who gives decent haircuts on Venus.

Solutions	Results
1. They ask the farmer where the nearest haircutter is.	1. The farmer screams and faints.
2. They ask the farmer's wife where the nearest haircutter is.	2. She screams and faints twice.

As you continue reading, keep paying attention to what Frank and Harry do to try and solve their problem. Underline each solution once and each result twice. At the end of the story, you will complete the problem-solution frame.

 Go on reading to see what happens.

48

"Oh dear," said Frank. "I'm afraid this saying 'hi' business is taking up too much time. Maybe we'd better just find a haircutter on our own."

"Good idea," said Harry.

And so they walked across the cornfield, and then across another cornfield, and then still another until they came to a small town.

They began walking down Main Street, saying a quick 'hi' to people (scream only). In return, everyone gave Frank and Harry a full 'hi' (scream and faint).

"These Earth people sure are a friendly bunch," noted Frank.

"Sure are," said Harry.

Finally they came to a shop with a sign that said, "Quick and Cheap Haircuts. No Appointment Needed."

Frank beamed over at Harry.

"Bingo!" he said, and they walked into the shop.

The only customer inside was a young boy. His face lit up when he saw Frank and Harry.

"Wow!" he said. "Where'd you guys come from?"

Just as Frank and Harry were about to respond, the haircutter turned around. He took one look at the two fat boys from Venus and screamed.

Frank and Harry **courteously** let out two short screams, turned to the boy, and said, "We're from Venus."

"Fantastic!" said the boy.

The haircutter had a different opinion.

He let out another scream—this one a little louder—and ran out of the shop, arms flailing and head rolling like a madman.

"Excuse me, sir," Frank called after the man. "When you're done exercising, would you mind cutting our hair?"

The haircutter picked up speed and was soon no longer in sight. Frank and Harry felt a tap on their tails. They turned around, and there stood the boy.

"I hate to tell you this," he said, "but I think Mr. Jones—the haircutter—will be taking the rest of the day off." Upon seeing Frank and Harry's faces drop with disappointment, the boy quickly added, "But don't worry. I'll cut your hair!"

"Would you really?" asked Harry.

"You bet!" said the boy, feeling terribly important. "C'mon over to these two chairs, and I'll have you done in a jiffy."

And so, during the next thirty minutes, Frank and Harry had their hair shampooed, rinsed, combed, cut, and dried. When it was all over, the boy handed Frank and Harry two large mirrors.

"Well?" he said, applying a finishing touch of gel. "What do you think?"

Frank and Harry were speechless. They looked **gorgeous**! Fantastic! Unbelievably handsome!

"How can we ever thank you?" they said to the boy.

"It was nothing at all," he said, flushed with pride.

Frank and Harry gave the boy their addresses and phone numbers. "If you ever get to Venus," they said, "please look us up. We'll treat you to a one-hundred-scoop ice-cream cone." They thanked the boy one more time and headed back to their spacecraft.

Just before they boarded, Frank said, "You know what, Harry?"

"What?" said Harry.

"That marvelous boy back there sure gave us a lot of good pointers on how to cut hair. I mean, who would have thought of using scissors to cut hair instead of yanking it out by hand?"

"Or," said Harry, "using warm water to wash a customer's hair instead of throwing a bucket of cold water on top of his head?"

"Yes," sighed Frank. "Our haircutters have a lot to learn." Frank paused for a moment. "Say, Harry, I've just had an idea. When we get back home, why don't you and I become haircutters? With all these new pointers we've gotten, we're bound to do a better job than the haircutters we have now. What do you think?"

"Frank, I think that is a *great* idea!" said Harry.

And so it was that Frank and Harry became Venus's first decent haircutters. And the whole planet was very, very happy. ●

Strategy Follow-up

Now complete this problem-solution frame for the second part of "Two Fat Boys from Venus." Use a separate sheet of paper if necessary. The problem box has been filled in for you.

What is the problem?
Two boys from Venus (Frank and Harry)
have come to Earth for haircuts.

Why is it a problem?
They can't find anyone who gives decent haircuts on Venus.

Solutions
Results

✓ Personal Checklist

Read each question and put a check (✓) in the correct box.

1. How well do you understand why everyone screams and faints when they see the two fat boys from Venus?
   - ☐ 3 (extremely well)
   - ☐ 2 (fairly well)
   - ☐ 1 (not well)

2. How well can you explain what makes this story funny?
   - ☐ 3 (extremely well)
   - ☐ 2 (fairly well)
   - ☐ 1 (not well)

3. How well were you able to use the information in Building Background to help you understand cultural differences?
   - ☐ 3 (extremely well)
   - ☐ 2 (fairly well)
   - ☐ 1 (not well)

4. How well were you able to answer the questions in the Vocabulary Builder?
   - ☐ 3 (extremely well)
   - ☐ 2 (fairly well)
   - ☐ 1 (not well)

5. How well were you able to complete the problem-solution frame in the Strategy Follow-up?
   - ☐ 3 (extremely well)
   - ☐ 2 (fairly well)
   - ☐ 1 (not well)

Vocabulary Check

Look back at the work you did in the Vocabulary Builder. Then answer each question by circling the correct letter.

1. The story says that the boys from Venus don't want to scare Earth's inhabitants. Which definition describes *inhabitants*?
   - a. people who visit a place
   - b. people who live in a place
   - c. people who scare a place

2. Which question or questions could you have answered with the word Venusian?
   - a. question a
   - b. questions a and d
   - c. questions a, b, and d

3. According to the story, Venus has abundant ice cream shops. What does *abundant* mean?
   - a. a very large number of
   - b. a very small number of
   - c. none at all

4. Which of the following is an example of the boys trying to act courteously?
   - a. screaming and falling on their backs
   - b. asking politely where they can get a haircut
   - c. both of the above

5. They young boy is a customer of Mr. Jones the haircutter. What is another word for *customer*?
   - a. boss
   - b. client
   - c. worker

Add the numbers that you just checked to get your Personal Checklist score. Fill in your score here. Then turn to page 205 and transfer your score onto Graph 1.

Check your answers with your teacher. Give yourself 1 point for each correct answer, and fill in your Vocabulary score here. Then turn to page 205 and transfer your score onto Graph 1.

Strategy Check

Review the problem-solution frame that you completed in the Strategy Follow-up. Then answer these questions:

1. What happens when Frank and Harry decide to find a haircutter on their own?
   a. They get lost and never end up finding one.
   b. They finally find a shop, but it is closed.
   c. They find a shop with quick, cheap haircuts.

2. What is the result when the boy in the shop gives Frank and Harry haircuts?
   a. They look gorgeous.
   b. They look ridiculous.
   c. Both of the above answers are correct.

3. What's the end result of the boys' problem?
   a. They stay on Earth and open a shop.
   b. They become haircutters in Mr. Jones's shop.
   c. They become the first decent haircutters on Venus.

4. Why do Frank and Harry become haircutters?
   a. because they got so many good pointers from the boy
   b. because they want to yank their customers' hair out
   c. because they want to throw cold water on customers' heads

5. If Frank and Harry didn't become haircutters themselves, how else might they have solved their problem?
   a. They might have screamed and fainted when they needed haircuts.
   b. They might have returned to Earth when they needed haircuts.
   c. They might have asked Mr. Jones to open a shop on Venus.

Comprehension Check

Review the story if necessary. Then answer these questions:

1. Why do Frank and Harry land on Earth?
   a. to take over the planet
   b. to get decent haircuts
   c. to learn how to lose weight

2. Why does the farmer scream and faint when he sees Frank and Harry?
   a. He is afraid of the boys.
   b. He doesn't like their haircuts.
   c. He thinks they're too fat.

3. What could cause Frank and Harry to think that people are saying "hi" when they scream and faint?
   a. It's the way Venusians say "hi" to each other too.
   b. It's the first thing Frank and Harry do when they see people on Earth.
   c. It's the first thing Earth people do when they see Frank and Harry.

4. Later in the story, why do Frank and Harry decide to scream but not faint?
   a. to say a quick "hi"
   b. to say a full "hi"
   c. not to say "hi" at all

5. Why do Frank and Harry think the haircutter is exercising when he sees them?
   a. because he's counting very loudly as he screams
   b. because he's running and flailing his arms
   c. because he's sweating like a madman

Check your answers with your teacher. Give yourself 1 point for each correct answer, and fill in your Strategy score here. Then turn to page 205 and transfer your score onto Graph 1.

Personal
Vocabulary
Strategy
Comprehension
TOTAL SCORE
✓ T

Check your answers with your teacher. Give yourself 1 point for each correct answer, and fill in your Comprehension score here. Then turn to page 205 and transfer your score onto Graph 1.

Personal
Vocabulary
Strategy
Comprehension
TOTAL SCORE
✓ T

Extending

Choose one or more of these activities:

DRAW AN ALIEN

Draw a picture of an alien that might come from another planet. Label the creature's body parts, items of clothing, or special gear. As you share your drawing with a partner or the class, explain why your alien is linked to a particular planet. For help in getting started, you might use *Drawing Aliens* and some of the books on planets that are listed on this page.

WRITE A SCIENCE FICTION STORY ABOUT YOUR ALIEN

Use a problem-solution frame to create a problem for your alien when it visits Earth for the first time. Then plan a few solutions and results, including the end result. Use your problem-solution frame to write a short science fiction story about your alien's adventures. If you need help getting ideas, you might look for the problems and solutions in some of the books listed on this page.

GIVE A NEWS REPORT

Choose a partner, and become on-the-scene reporters. In a "live" broadcast that you perform for a few classmates, explain what happened when two fat Venusian boys paid a visit to Earth. Give a detailed account of the highlights of the day. If you'd like, include brief interviews with some of the people who saw or spoke with the Venusians.

Resources

Books

2095 by Jon Scieszka. Copyright © 1997 by Puffin.

Alien Invasion from Hollyweird by John Peel. Copyright © 1999 by Tor Books.

Aliens Ate My Homework by Bruce Coville. Copyright © 1993 by Minstrel Books.

Aliens in the Sky by Christopher Pike. Copyright © 1996 by Minstrel Books.

Draw Alien Fantasies, by Damon J. Reinagle. Copyright © 1996 by Peel Productions.

Facts on File: Stars and Planets Atlas by Jan Ridpath. Copyright © 1998 by Facts on File, Inc.

Night of the Aliens by Dayle Campbell Gaetz. Copyright © 1995 by Roussan Publishers.

Venus by Muriel Schloss. Copyright © 1996 by Franklin Watts.

Learning New Words

VOCABULARY

From Lesson 1
- dirtiest
  muddiest

- gleamed
  sparkled

- speck
  spot

Synonyms

A synonym is a word that means the same thing—or close to the same thing—as another word. For example, author Helen Ketteman uses the synonyms *dirtiest* and *muddiest* to describe the town of Mudville when Shoeshine Whittaker arrives there. She uses *gleamed* and *sparkled* to describe what Mudville looked like after Shoeshine rubbed and scrubbed it.

Draw a line from each word in Column 1 to its synonym in Column 2.

Column 1	Column 2
doubt	boring
dull	rule
explore	question
law	faithful
loyal	examine

Antonyms

From Lesson 1
- clean
  dusty

- down
  up

- dulling
  shining

An antonym is a word that means the opposite of another word. For example, Helen Ketteman uses the antonyms *dusty* and *clean* to describe Mudville before and after Shoeshine Whittaker's arrival.

Draw a line from each word in Column 1 to its antonym in Column 2.

Column 1	Column 2
friend	end
joyful	sorrowful
beginning	cool
filthy	spotless
warm	enemy

Multiple-Meaning Words

VOCABULARY

From Lesson 2
- fair
- toe

From Lesson 3
- orders

A single word can have more than one meaning. As you learned in Lesson 2, the word *toe* can refer to a part of the foot, a dance performed on the toes, or a West India gherkin pickle. To figure out which meaning of *toe* the author was using, you had to use context. Context is the information surrounding a word or situation that helps you understand it.

When you read "The Big Toe Contest" you used context to figure out that Hayden's meaning for toe was "part of the foot." But in the context of the contest, *toe* referred to a West India gherkin pickle. Then at the end of the selection, Hayden mentioned that his aunt's dance troupe needed toe dancers. In that context, *toe* meant "a dance performed on the toes."

Now use context to figure out the correct meaning of each underlined word. Circle the letter of the correct meaning.

1. Brad and Brenda watched their favorite actress perform in a play last night.
   a. dramatic presentation

   b. thing done for sport

2. I replaced the batteries in my alarm clock when it stopped running.

   a. going faster than walking

   b. working or operating

3. My mother squeezed our little car into a tight parking space.

   a. length of time

   b. spot or place

4. Both sides of the debate team argued their points very well.

   a. main ideas

   b. tiny dots

Put the Brolly in the Boot and Let's Go

bangers

biscuits

bonnet

boot

chemist

crisps

loo

lorry

surgery

tea

valise

Building Background

Put the brolly in the boot? You're probably asking yourself, "What does *that* mean?" Believe it or not, the words in the title "Put the Brolly in the Boot and Let's Go" are all in English—British English. You may have noticed that people in various parts of the United States and the world sometimes speak English differently than you do. When you're trying to understand words that you've never heard before—even words spoken in English—you must rely on context to help you break the "language barrier."

Read the following sentences, and see if they provide enough context to help you figure out what a brolly is:

"We'll just put your valise and my brolly in the boot and be on our way. . . ." Uncle Brian stowed the suitcase and the umbrella in the car's trunk.

By using context, you probably figured out that a brolly is either a suitcase or an umbrella. And maybe you noticed that there is some similarity between the words *brolly* and *umbrella*. That probably gave you even more clues. Do you know what a brolly is now?

Vocabulary Builder

1. The words in Column 1 on page 57 are all British terms. Do you know what any of them mean? If you do, draw a line from each one to its definition in Column 2.

2. If you don't know what some of the terms mean, find them as you read the story. Use context to try to figure them out. Then match them to their definitions in Column 2.

3. Save your work. You will use it again in the Vocabulary Check.

COLUMN 1	COLUMNN 2
bangers	hood of a car ✓
biscuits	suitcase ✓
bonnet	trunk of a car ✓
boot	truck ✓
chemist	sausages served with mashed potatoes ✓
crisps	snacks served in the late afternoon ✓
loo	doctor's office ✓
lorry	druggist ✓
surgery	cookies ✓
tea	restroom ✓
valise	potato chips ✓

Strategy Builder

Comparing and Contrasting While You Read

- Authors often compare and contrast things when they write. **Comparing** means looking at how two or more things are similar, or alike. **Contrasting** means looking at how two or more things are different.

- Making a **comparison chart** while you read can help you keep track of how things are alike and different. For example, if you were reading an article about soccer and American football, your comparison chart might look like this:

	Soccer	American Football
Equipment	• soccer ball (round)	• American football (oval shaped)
Playing Areas	• outdoor field • indoor stadium	• outdoor field • indoor stadium
Scoring	• goal = 1 point	• touchdown = 6 points • conversion = 1 point • field goal = 3 points • safety = 2 points

- The chart helps you easily compare and contrast the equipment, playing areas, and scoring in each sport. For example, you can see that both football and soccer can be played indoors or outdoors. You also can see that there are four ways to score in football, but there is only one way to score in soccer.

Put the Brolly in the Boot and Let's Go

by Kathryn Slattery

As you read the first part of this story, look for how things in Great Britain compare and contrast with things in the United States. Use context to figure out any unfamiliar words.

Jenny's stomach tightened as she looked around London's Heathrow Airport. She was glad that the airline hostess was there to help. It was her first trip outside the United States. At least her parents had been right about her not having to learn a foreign language. The signs overhead were in English.

Suddenly Jenny saw Uncle Brian waving his umbrella. His eyes twinkled as he shook Jenny's hand. "Welcome to Great Britain," he said.

The air hostess checked Uncle Brian's identification. "Have fun, and eat plenty of **bangers**!" she called as she left.

"Come on. First, we'll grab a trolley; then we can ride the lift down to the ground floor and claim your baggage."

Jenny was confused, and they hadn't even left the airport! She followed Uncle Brian and the luggage cart to the elevator. Soon they had Jenny's suitcase and were outside.

"My car's next to the **lorry**." Uncle Brian pointed to a sedan parked next to a delivery truck. "We'll just put your **valise** and my brolly in the **boot** and be on our way. I checked under the **bonnet** this morning so we'll have a smooth ride."

Uncle Brian stowed the suitcase and the umbrella in the car's trunk. Jenny slid into the front seat. The steering wheel was on the wrong side!

On the drive home, Jenny gripped the edge of the seat. She felt like Alice in Wonderland; everything was just a bit off. "Relax," Uncle Brian said, smiling. "Everyone in England drives on this side. For us it's the right side, even if it is on the left."

"Gee, Uncle Brian," Jenny whispered, "Mom said you would speak English and you do, but not quite."

"Tell you what. Let me know when you don't understand something, and I'll translate."

Jenny nodded.

Stop here for the Strategy Break.

Strategy Break

If you were to make a comparison chart for this story so far, it might look like this:

	Life in Great Britain	Life in the United States
Spoken language	• English	• English
Written language	• English	• English
Transportation	• People drive on the left-hand side of the road. • The steering wheel is on the right-hand side of the car.	• People drive on the right-hand side of the road. • The steering wheel is on the left-hand side of the car.

As you already know, the words for many things are different in each country. Take a look back at the Vocabulary Builder. If you did not correctly match the British terms *bangers, lorry, valise, boot,* and *bonnet* with their American definitions, go back and do that now. Then read the rest of the story. In the Strategy Follow-up, you will continue to compare and contrast life in Great Britain and life in the United States.

 Go on reading to see what happens.

Soon they were driving down a narrow road with houses and shops on each side.

"That's my **surgery**," Uncle Brian said, pointing, "and the **chemist** is right next to it."

Jenny thought her uncle was a regular doctor, but maybe he was a scientist too. "Do you experiment with new medicines and then go next door when you need to operate on your patients?"

Uncle Brian chuckled. "A surgery is a doctor's office in England. And at the chemist's they sell only medicines and such." Uncle Brian turned the car into a gravel drive. "Here we are. Your cousin Heather should be home from cricket practice by now. She's really excited to meet you."

A girl with red hair came running out of the house.

"Heather, slow down," Uncle Brian said.

Heather grinned. She grabbed Jenny's bag. "Come on. You're going to share my room. It'll be brilliant!"

Jenny followed Heather as she bumped the heavy suitcase upstairs.

"My room is right here, past the **loo**," Heather said. She led the way into a bedroom right next to the bathroom.

Even the bathroom has a different name, thought Jenny.

Uncle Brian called from downstairs. "Heather, bring your cousin down. Mum wants to say hello."

Aunt Sylvia greeted Jenny seriously. "Welcome to England," she said. "Are you ready for **tea**?"

"Yes, thank you," Jenny answered, remembering her mother's instructions to be polite. "But could I have something to eat too? I'm really hungry. I didn't eat much on the plane."

Aunt Sylvia smiled. "This is afternoon tea, Jenny," she said, pointing at the dining room table laid with all kinds of food. There were cookies and little sandwiches with the crusts cut off. There were big, fluffy **biscuits**, pots of jam and butter, and a bowl of some kind of dessert topped with whipped cream. "What would you like to eat?" she asked.

"A biscuit, please, and some of those little sandwiches."

Aunt Sylvia served Jenny two triangular sandwiches and passed the plate of cookies.

Jenny took a cookie and asked timidly, "Could I try a biscuit too, please?"

Aunt Sylvia looked puzzled. Heather began to giggle, and Uncle Brian laughed out loud. "Jenny, I'm sorry. I keep forgetting." He turned to Heather. "Jenny is having trouble understanding our English. Lots of things have different names in America. In America biscuits are like our scones. What we call biscuits, they call cookies."

"Just when I think I understand, then someone says something strange," said Jenny. "It's rather like a puzzle."

"I'll help you," Heather offered. "We can make it a game." She got right into the spirit of being a teacher. "That's trifle; under the cream there's cake and custard. For dinner Mum's making my favorite—bangers. That's sausages and mash."

"Speaking of potatoes," added Uncle Brian, "we call French fries chips and what you call potato chips, we call **crisps**."

"When we were in the States when Heather was a baby, I had to learn lots of new words." Aunt Sylvia thought for a minute. "There was the word *diapers* for nappies. A cot was called a crib. The Americans said baby buggy instead of pram. When Heather lost her dummy and we tried to buy a new one, the sales clerk just laughed. 'Call it a pacifier,' she told us."

"I need a pencil and paper," Jenny said. "I'll never remember it all!"

"Come on. Let's go into the living room." Heather was excited. "Jenny can teach me the American words for things we hear on the telly!"

Jenny grinned. "I know what that is—the television."

"Brilliant!" Uncle Brian declared. ●

Strategy Follow-up

Complete the comparison chart below with information from the second part of the story. Go back and skim the story if you need to.

	Life in Great Britain	Life in the United States
What a chemist does		
What people have during tea		
What baby things are called		

✓Personal Checklist

Read each question and put a check (✓) in the correct box.

1. How well were you able to use the information in Building Background to understand Jenny's problem?
   - ☐ 3 (extremely well)
   - ☐ 2 (fairly well)
   - ☐ 1 (not well)

2. How well were you able to understand why Jenny felt like Alice in Wonderland on the drive home?
   - ☐ 3 (extremely well)
   - ☐ 2 (fairly well)
   - ☐ 1 (not well)

3. How well were you able to use context to figure out the British terms?
   - ☐ 3 (extremely well)
   - ☐ 2 (fairly well)
   - ☐ 1 (not well)

4. In the Vocabulary Builder, how many British and American terms were you able to match correctly?
   - ☐ 3 (8–11 terms)
   - ☐ 2 (4–7 terms)
   - ☐ 1 (0–3 terms)

5. How well were you able to complete the comparison chart in the Strategy Follow-up?
   - ☐ 3 (extremely well)
   - ☐ 2 (fairly well)
   - ☐ 1 (not well)

Vocabulary Check

Look back at the work you did in the Vocabulary Builder. Then answer each question by circling the correct letter.

1. Which context clue helped you figure out exactly what bangers are?
   a. "Have fun, and eat plenty of bangers!"
   b. "Mum's making my favorite—bangers."
   c. "That's sausages and mash."

2. What is a British dummy called in the States?
   a. diaper
   b. pacifier
   c. crib

3. Which match is correct?
   a. British surgery = American surgery
   b. British surgery = American doctor's office
   c. British surgery = American doctor

4. Which of the following would be served during British tea?
   a. scones and jam
   b. bangers and mash
   c. peanut butter-and-jelly sandwiches

5. What are French fries called in Great Britain?
   a. chips
   b. crisps
   c. potato chips

Add the numbers that you just checked to get your Personal Checklist score. Fill in your score here. Then turn to page 205 and transfer your score onto Graph 1.

Check your answers with your teacher. Give yourself 1 point for each correct answer, and fill in your Vocabulary score here. Then turn to page 205 and transfer your score onto Graph 1.

Strategy Check

Review the comparison chart that you completed in the Strategy Follow-up. Then answer these questions.

1. What does an American chemist do?
   a. studies different substances and experiments with them
   b. studies different patients and operates on them
   c. sells different kinds of medicines

2. Why does Jenny think that her uncle experiments on his patients?
   a. because American chemists do experiments
   b. because he says he's next to a chemist
   c. because of both reasons above

3. What is different about having tea in Britain and having tea in the States?
   a. In Britain you usually have just tea, but in the States you eat lots of food with it.
   b. In the States you usually have just tea, but in Britain you eat lots of food with it.
   c. Nothing—having tea is the same in both countries.

4. How are the names of baby things different in Britain and the States?
   a. An American baby buggy is called a brolly in Britain.
   b. British nappies are called diapers in the States.
   c. Both of the above answers are correct.

5. If you asked for a biscuit in Britain, what would you get?
   a. a scone
   b. a sandwich
   c. a cookie

Comprehension Check

Review the story if necessary. Then answer these questions:

1. Why is Jenny so confused in this story?
   a. Several British terms are unfamiliar to Jenny.
   b. They don't speak English in Great Britain.
   c. Jenny doesn't know a foreign language.

2. Which of the following differences is not related to language?
   a. calling an umbrella a brolly
   b. driving on the other side of the street
   c. saying Mum instead of Mom

3. Why does Jenny ask for something to eat with her tea?
   a. She thinks tea is only something to drink.
   b. She wants a full American dinner with her tea.
   c. She wants to be polite, even though she is full.

4. What does Heather mean when she says, "You're going to share my room. It'll be brilliant!"
   a. It will be great fun to share her room.
   b. Her room will be very shiny.
   c. Sharing a room will be very intelligent.

5. When Jenny arrives, Heather is at cricket practice. In the context of this story, what does cricket mean?
   a. a small, low wooden stool
   b. a leaping insect related to the grasshopper
   c. an outdoor game played with wickets

Check your answers with your teacher. Give yourself 1 point for each correct answer, and fill in your Strategy score here. Then turn to page 205 and transfer your score onto Graph 1.

Personal	
Vocabulary	
Strategy	
Comprehension	
TOTAL SCORE	

✓ T

Check your answers with your teacher. Give yourself 1 point for each correct answer, and fill in your Comprehension score here. Then turn to page 205 and transfer your score onto Graph 1.

Personal	
Vocabulary	
Strategy	
Comprehension	
TOTAL SCORE	

✓ T

Extending

Choose one or both of these activities:

PLAN A MENU FOR AFTERNOON TEA

Using some of the resources on this page or ones that you find yourself, find out what foods are typically eaten during afternoon tea in Britain. Then, with a group of classmates, plan a menu for an afternoon tea. If you can, find recipes for some of the foods on your menu. Prepare the foods, and then share them with the class during your own afternoon tea.

READ ALOUD TO YOUNGER STUDENTS

Choose a book written by a British author, such as James Herriot or Michael Bond. Prepare to read the book to a group of younger students. Make sure you understand any unfamiliar words or phrases so that you can explain them as you read. Use the resources listed on this page to help you find British books and terms.

Resources

Books

A Taste of Britain by Roz Denny. Copyright © 1998 by Thomson Learning.

Oscar, Cat-About-Town by James Herriot. Copyright © 1993 by St. Martin's Press.

Paddington at Large by Michael Bond. Copyright © 1998 by Houghton Mifflin Co.

Great Britain by Philip Steele. Copyright © 1994 by Crestwood House.

Getting to Know Britain: People, Places by Moira Butterfield. Copyright © 1994 by Barrons Juveniles.

Understanding British English by Margaret Moore. Copyright © 1997 by Carol Publishing Group.

NTC's Dictionary of British Slang and Colloquial Expressions: The Most Practical Reference for the Informal Expressions of British English by James Ewart. Copyright © 1998 by NTC/Contemporary Publishing Company.

Web Site

www.globalfriends.com/html/world_tour/england/england.htm
Learn all about England, including more British words and phrases.

abscess

accompanist

ambitious

aria

flourish

lanced

precious

recitative

trill

unanimous

Descriptive Words

Medical Words

Music Words

LESSON 7
The Contest

Building Background

Marian Anderson was born in Philadelphia, Pennsylvania, in 1897. She began singing in church choirs when she was just a child. After graduating from high school, she performed in both Europe and the United States.

Because she was black, Marian's career often was affected by racism. For example, in 1939 the Daughters of the American Revolution would not allow Marian to perform at Constitution Hall in Washington, D.C. Things turned out well after all, however: She sang at the Lincoln Memorial instead—to a crowd of more than 75,000 people!

Marian Anderson's talent was so great that the famous conductor Arturo Toscanini praised her voice as one "that comes once in a hundred years." In addition to her many singing accomplishments, Marian wrote her autobiography, *My Lord, What a Morning,* in 1956; became a U.S. delegate to the United Nations in 1958; and won the UN peace prize in 1977. Marian Anderson died in 1993.

Vocabulary Builder

1. Before you begin reading "The Contest," read the vocabulary words in the margin. Write any of the words that you already know on the appropriate clipboards.

2. Later, as you read "The Contest," find the vocabulary words you don't know. Read them in context, and decide what they mean. Then write the words on the appropriate clipboards.

3. If using context doesn't help you figure out what a word means, look it up in a dictionary. If the dictionary gives more than one meaning for the word, be sure to choose the one that is used in the selection.

4. Save your work. You will refer to it again in the Vocabulary Check.

Strategy Builder

How to Read a Biographical Sketch

- A **biography** is the story of a real person's life, written by someone else. A **biographical sketch** is the story of a part of a real person's life. "The Contest" is a biographical sketch that describes what happened to Marian Anderson when she tried out for a chance to sing at Lewisohn Stadium in New York. This biographical sketch is taken from Janet Stevenson's biography of Anderson called *Singing to the World.*

- Biographical sketches describe events in the order in which they happened. That order is called time order, or **sequence**. To make the sequence as clear as possible, writers often use words called **signal words**. Some examples of signal words are *first, then, after that, a few days later,* and *at that moment.*

- A biographical sketch is always written in the **third-person point of view**. That means that the narrator tells the subject's story using words such as *he, she, his, her, they,* and *theirs.*

- The paragraph below is from a biographical sketch about a boy named Jonathan. They describe what he did before school one morning. Notice the signal words, which are underlined.

> Jonathan woke up <u>this morning</u> and got out of bed. His dog was waiting for him at the kitchen table. It was wagging its tail and barking. It looked pretty funny. <u>Before breakfast</u> Jonathan watched the news on TV. There was a story about a film being made in his town. <u>After he ate breakfast</u> he brushed his teeth. <u>Next</u> he got dressed and combed his hair. It was picture day at school, and he wanted to look nice. <u>When he left the house</u>, he caught the bus. <u>On the ride to school</u> he studied for a test.

If you wanted to show the sequence of events in the paragraphs above, you could use a **sequence chain** like this one:

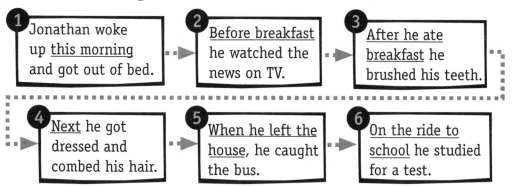

The Contest

by Janet Stevenson

As you read the first part of "The Contest," apply the strategies that you just learned. Notice the underlined signal words. They will give you a more exact picture of when things happened.

Marian Anderson was one of the greatest concert singers of the 20th century. Before achieving worldwide fame, she took part in many voice contests. In 1925 her voice teacher entered her in a contest for an appearance at Lewisohn Stadium in New York City. The biographical sketch you are about to read describes the events leading up to Anderson's final round of tryouts.

Every one of the contestants—and there were 300 of them—had an **accompanist**, and most had a teacher with them too. The crowd filled the whole ground floor of Aeolian Hall.

At the appointed hour, the rules were announced over a public address system from the balcony, where the judges sat—heard but not seen. They explained that there was not time for each contestant to sing all the material he or she had prepared. The judges would listen to what they felt to be a fair sample. Then a clicker would sound. The singer was to stop and leave the stage.

"Pay no attention," Mr. Boghetti whispered in Marian's ear. "If they stop you, pretend you don't hear. Go on to the end. Be sure you get in that final **trill**."

"Go on singing when they tell me to stop?"

Marian was appalled at such boldness, but Mr. Boghetti believed in boldness.

"Not for everybody, maybe. But for you. You must insist that they hear you out."

Marian said nothing, but she didn't believe she could do what he was asking. Hard as it was to disobey her teacher, it would be harder to disobey the unseen judges.

Meanwhile she had drawn a number and was waiting her turn. By the time it came near, several other singers had sung her Donizetti **aria**. Not one of them had got to the final trill. Each time the clicker cut short their song, Marian winced. Each time she winced, Mr. Boghetti glared a warning at her.

"What if I skip the **recitative** and start with the aria itself?" she whispered.

He shook his head. "Sing it all. Make them listen!"

The next contestants got only a minute or two apiece. It was her turn.

She began with the half-spoken recitative, though it seemed a waste of **precious** time. She could feel her teacher's hypnotic eye on her, reminding her of his command. She was expecting at any instant the sound of the clicker and the awful decision—which command to disobey?

But the clicker didn't sound.

Maybe she didn't hear it. (Her ears had felt a little dull since her last ducking in the Y pool.) She was well into the aria now! Singing as if each note might be the last—as indeed it might! On and on to the great final trill! She sang it through to the last beautiful **flourish**!

There was a second of dead silence. Then applause broke out all over Aeolian Hall.

An angry voice on the loud speaker reminded the audience that applause was forbidden. <u>Then</u> it asked Marian whether she had another song.

She sang one of her English songs and went back to her seat.

"Did the clicker sound?" she asked Mr. Boghetti.

"No! You are the only one who has finished the aria! Not to speak of a second song!"

They left soon afterwards to catch the train back to Philadelphia. Mr. Boghetti was elated by her success, but as always he found things that could be improved. He talked about them <u>all the way home</u>, which gave Marian a change to relax and become aware of something very peculiar about one of her ears.

It was not so much pain as a sort of numbness. She said nothing about it. She had never mentioned the swimming lessons to Mr. Boghetti and she suspected that he was not going to approve. Not if the trouble in her ear had anything to do with them.

Perhaps it would be better to give up swimming.

<u>Two days later</u> Mr. Boghetti called her on the phone.

"You have won!"

"Won?"

"You are one of 16 who will sing in the semifinals. Four will be chosen from them."

 Stop here for the Strategy Break.

Strategy Break

If you were to arrange the main events in this selection so far, they might look like this:

1 At the appointed hour, the rules are announced. ▶ **2** Mr. Boghetti tells Marian to keep singing if they tell her to stop. ▶ **3** Marian makes it through her whole song!

4 Then she is asked to sing another one. ▶ **5** All the way home, she notices a numbness in one of her ears. ▶ **6** Two days later, Marian finds out she has made it to the semifinals.

As you continue reading, keep paying attention to the order of events. Also keep looking for signal words, and underline them. At the end of this selection you will use them to create a sequence chain of your own.

➡ **Go on reading.**

So it was back to work in the muggy heat. Marian was almost tempted to go back to the Y pool, just to cool off a little, but her ear still felt strange. She thought once of going to a doctor, but it got no worse, and she really had no time to spare.

On the second trip to New York, Mr. Boghetti was full of **ambitious** hopes. He was talking about how he would coach Marian for the Lewisohn Stadium appearance, assuming that she would win today's round, and go on to win the semifinals. Marian wished she could share his enthusiasm, but she felt wooden beside him.

In fact she felt worse than wooden. Her ear was beginning to hurt.

She had thought when she got up this morning that there was something stuck in it. Perhaps it was one of the little cotton plugs she had used to keep the water out while she swam. She tried pulling it out, first with her fingers, then with tweezers, but working at it made it worse.

By the time they got to Aeolian Hall, she had a real old-fashioned earache. Not unbearable yet, but getting worse.

"It won't be so long today," Mr. Boghetti said cheerfully. "There are only 16 contestants. You may be one of the first."

Marian hoped so. She was not sure now long she could hold out. But Mr. Boghetti was right; she was called after only a half hour's wait.

She had to sing her aria and both her other songs. As soon as she was through, Mr. Boghetti took her back to his studio to rest until train time.

"Why do you look so discouraged?" he asked. "You did well. Very well!"

Marian was tempted to tell him that it was not discouragement he saw on her face. But it had got too bad to talk about at all. She felt as if there were some horrible growth deep inside her ear. Her hearing was affected. What if it turned out to be permanent? Beethoven had gone deaf, and he had gone on composing and conducting, but who ever heard of a deaf singer?

The phone rang and Mr. Boghetti answered it.

"What? . . . Are you sure? . . . All right, all right!"

He turned back to Marian with a dazed look, which could be the shock of joy or the shock of defeat.

"There are to be no finals," he said. "It is **unanimous**. You will sing on August 25th at Lewisohn Stadium!"

At that moment Marian was wondering whether she would ever sing anywhere again.

But the growth in her ear was only an **abscess**. As soon as it was **lanced** and the pressure relieved, the pain began to ease.

"Will I be deaf?" she asked the doctor.

"Not if you take care of yourself, and stay out of swimming pools for the rest of the summer."

Orders she didn't mind obeying for the rest of that summer and several summers to come! ●

Strategy Follow-up

Now create a sequence chain for the second part of this selection. Use a separate sheet of paper if you need to. Don't forget to use (and underline) as many signal words as you can.

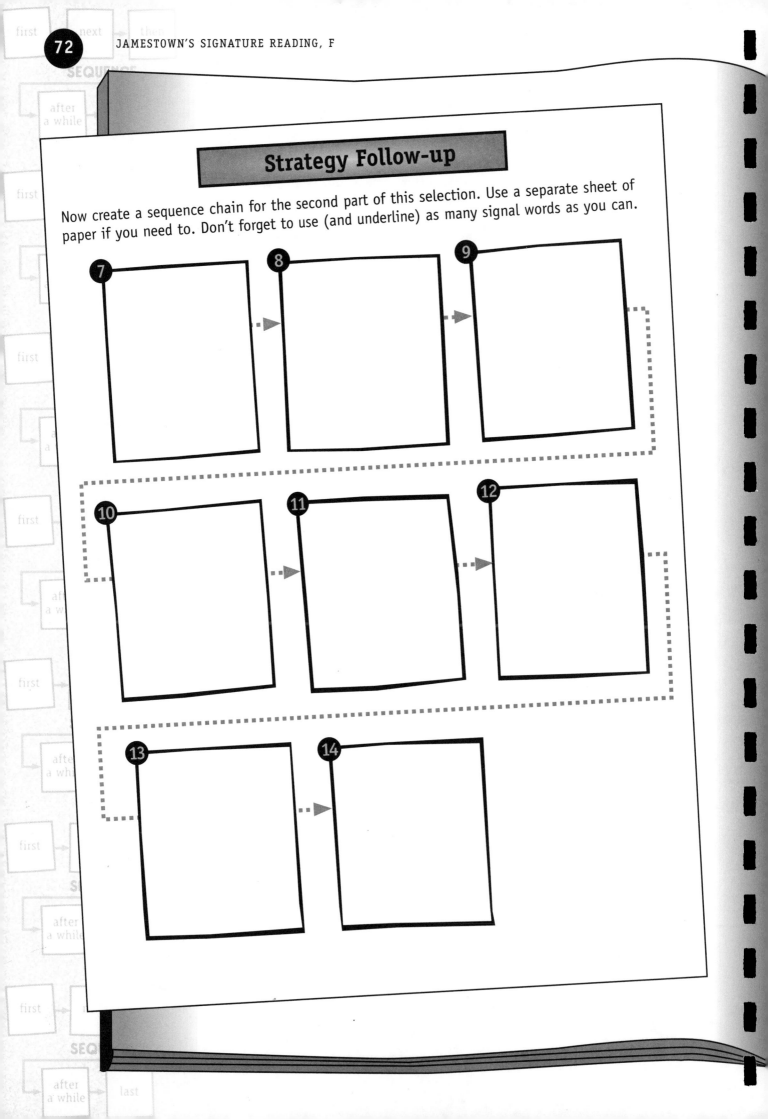

✓Personal Checklist

Read each question and put a check (✓) in the correct box.

1. How well do you understand what happened in "The Contest"?
   - ☐ 3 (extremely well)
   - ☐ 2 (fairly well)
   - ☐ 1 (not well)

2. How well do you understand the personalities and motivations of Marian and Mr. Boghetti?
   - ☐ 3 (extremely well)
   - ☐ 2 (fairly well)
   - ☐ 1 (not well)

3. How well were you able to use the information in Building Background to help you predict the outcome of Marian's tryouts?
   - ☐ 3 (extremely well)
   - ☐ 2 (fairly well)
   - ☐ 1 (not well)

4. By the time you finished reading "The Contest," how many vocabulary words were you able to write on the appropriate clipboards?
   - ☐ 3 (8–10 words)
   - ☐ 2 (4–7 words)
   - ☐ 1 (0–3 words)

5. How well were you able to complete the sequence chain in the Strategy Follow-up?
   - ☐ 3 (extremely well)
   - ☐ 2 (fairly well)
   - ☐ 1 (not well)

Vocabulary Check

Look back at the work you did in the Vocabulary Builder. Then answer each question by circling the correct letter.

1. On which clipboard did you write the words *ambitious, precious,* and *unanimous*?
   a. Descriptive Words
   b. Medical Words
   c. Music Words

2. Every contestant in the first round of tryouts has an accompanist. Who or what is an *accompanist*?
   a. a person who coaches a singer during a contest
   b. a person who plays an instrument to back up a singer
   c. an instrument that a person uses to back up a singer

3. Which vocabulary word were you able to figure out by using the context clue "half-spoken"?
   a. trill
   b. flourish
   c. recitative

4. Which meaning of the word *flourish* fits this selection?
   a. a showy trill or passage of music
   b. a being in the best time of one's life or activity
   c. an ornamental curve in one's handwriting

5. The judges' choice of Marian as the contest winner is unanimous. What does *unanimous* mean?
   a. agreed upon by everyone
   b. agreed upon by no one
   c. decided by only one judge

Add the numbers that you just checked to get your Personal Checklist score. Fill in your score here. Then turn to page 205 and transfer your score onto Graph 1.

Personal
Vocabulary
Strategy
Comprehension
TOTAL SCORE
✓ T

Check your answers with your teacher. Give yourself 1 point for each correct answer, and fill in your Vocabulary score here. Then turn to page 205 and transfer your score onto Graph 1.

Personal
Vocabulary
Strategy
Comprehension
TOTAL SCORE
✓ T

Strategy Check

Review the sequence chain that you completed in the Strategy Follow-up. Then answer these questions:

1. Which sentence could you have written for Event 7?
   a. By the time she gets to Aeolian Hall, Marian has a real earache.
   b. Marian is called to sing after only a half-hour's wait.
   c. On the second trip to New York, Marian's ear is beginning to hurt.

2. Which phrase is not an example of signal words?
   a. but it had got too bad
   b. as soon as she was through
   c. at that moment

3. What do Marian and Mr. Boghetti do after Marian finishes her semifinal tryout?
   a. They go back to Mr. Boghetti's studio so Marian can rest.
   b. They go to the train station to wait for the train.
   c. They go to Lewisohn Stadium to prepare for her appearance.

4. When does Marian have her abscess lanced?
   a. before the semifinal round of the contest
   b. during the semifinal round of the contest
   c. after the semifinal round of the contest

5. Which sentence could be the last event on your sequence chain?
   a. Mr. Boghetti tells Marian that there will be no finals.
   b. The doctor tells Marian to stay out of pools for the rest of the summer.
   c. As soon as Marian's abscess is lanced, the pain begins to ease.

Comprehension Check

Review the selection if necessary. Then answer these questions:

1. How many people compete in the first round of the contest?
   a. 30
   b. 100
   c. 300

2. How many people compete in the semifinal round?
   a. 4
   b. 16
   c. 30

3. Why is there no final round to the contest?
   a. The judges all agree after the semifinal round that Marian is the winner of the contest.
   b. Everyone but Marian drops out of the contest, so she wins the final round.
   c. There actually is a final round, but Marian is too ill to compete in it.

4. Why doesn't Marian tell Mr. Boghetti that she is taking swimming lessons?
   a. She doesn't think he will approve of her taking them.
   b. She is afraid he will blame her earache on them.
   c. Both of the above answers are correct.

5. Which words best describe Marian?
   a. happy and carefree
   b. obedient and hard-working
   c. bored and disgusted

Check your answers with your teacher. Give yourself 1 point for each correct answer, and fill in your Strategy score here. Then turn to page 205 and transfer your score onto Graph 1.

Personal
Vocabulary
Strategy
Comprehension
TOTAL SCORE
✓ T

Check your answers with your teacher. Give yourself 1 point for each correct answer, and fill in your Comprehension score here. Then turn to page 205 and transfer your score onto Graph 1.

Personal
Vocabulary
Strategy
Comprehension
TOTAL SCORE
✓ T

Extending

Choose one or more of these activities:

SUMMARIZE THE SELECTION

Use the vocabulary words and your sequence chain to summarize what happened in "The Contest." Try to use as many vocabulary words as possible in your summary. Also use as many signal words as possible to help clarify the order of events. Then share your summary with a partner. Can he or she follow the order of events easily? Make any revisions to your summary that you feel are necessary.

RESEARCH MARIAN ANDERSON'S LIFE

Work alone or with a group of classmates to find out more about Marian Anderson's life and career. Use some of the resources on this page if you'd like. Report your findings orally or in writing.

RESPOND TO ANDERSON'S WORK

Listen to a recording of Marian Anderson's work, and choose the song that most appeals to you. (For ideas, see the recordings listed on this page.) Respond to the song in one of the following ways:

words—write a poem, song, descriptive paragraph, or critique

pictures—work in water colors, oils, or a medium of your choice

shapes—make a sculpture or a three-dimensional scene, using the medium of your choice

music—play or sing a song that you or someone else composed

movement—perform a dance to the song you have chosen

Resources

Books

What I Had Was Singing: The Story of Marian Anderson by Jeri Ferris. Copyright ©1994 by First Avenue Edition.

Marian Anderson by Anne Tedards and Martina S. Horner. Copyright © 1989 by Chelsea House Publishing.

Web Sites

http://www.classicalmus.com
This site includes a substantial biography on Anderson, as well as a discography.

http://www.ubl.com/
This site includes a short biography, a discography, a feature that you can download in order to listen to selected cuts from her recordings, and on-line shopping.

Music

He's Got the Whole World in His Hands by Marian Anderson. Copyright © 1994 by RCA Records. (spirituals)

Great Voices of the Century by Marian Anderson. Copyright © 1996 by Memoir Records. (opera)

LESSON 8

The Fabulous Miss Bly

Building Background

In 1890, New York held a parade in honor of Elizabeth Cochrane. Was she a movie star? an astronaut? a visiting princess? No, she was a newspaper reporter. She was about 23 years old. And she had just circled the globe in 72 days. Elizabeth Cochrane changed her name to Nellie Bly when she became a reporter. You will read about her adventurous life and how she tried to help people, especially the mentally ill, in the following selection.

Vocabulary Builder

article

editor

editorial

published

reporter

reports

topic

1. The vocabulary words in the margin are all related to newspaper publishing. Some of the words may be familiar to you. Find those words in the statements below. If a word is used correctly, write **C** on the line beside it. If a word is used incorrectly, write **I**.

2. Then, as you read the selection, use context clues to figure out any of the vocabulary words you don't know. Go back and write **C** or **I** next to those sentences. Double-check your earlier work, and make any necessary changes.

3. Save your work. You will use it again in the Vocabulary Check.

___ a. James drew an **article** for his daily comic strip.

___ b. An **editor** is a person who runs a high school.

___ c. Marcia wrote an **editorial** on her opinion of computers.

___ d. Mr. Gardner **published** his first book last year.

___ e. A **reporter** burst into the store to arrest the thief.

___ f. Sam Hill wrote a series of **reports** on life in big cities.

___ g. Jason rubbed a **topic** cream on his bruised knee.

Strategy Builder

How to Read a Biography

- In Lesson 7 you learned that a **biographical sketch** tells about a specific time in a real person's life. In this lesson you will read a biography. A **biography** tells about a real person's *entire* life, as written by someone else.

- The events in most biographies are told in the **sequence**, or time order, in which they happened. When you read Marian Anderson's biographical sketch, you used a sequence chain to record the order of events. As you read Nellie Bly's biography, however, you will use a time line. A **time line** is more effective when you are looking at a person's entire life, since it allows you to show a much longer period of time.

- Read the following paragraphs from a biography of Dorthea Dix.

> Dorthea Dix was born in 1802 in what is now Maine. Her early life was difficult. This may have led to her later goal of helping others who were unable to help themselves. In 1841 she began to work on improving the treatment of mentally ill people and prisoners. Three years later she moved to New Jersey and worked to build a state asylum for the mentally ill. About a year later, Dix wrote a book about the work she did with prisoners.
>
> In 1861 Dix was chosen to be the Superintendent of Army Nurses during the Civil War. She was not very good at this job. Five years later she decided to return to her first cause, helping the mentally ill. Dix died in 1887 at the age of 85. The New Jersey State Lunatic Asylum stands as a tribute to her life's work.

- If you wanted to create a time line to show the major events in Dorthea Dix's life, it would look like this:

The Fabulous Miss Bly

As you read this biography, note the dates and important events in Nellie Bly's life. Be careful—not all of the dates are presented in order.

In the 1800s, many young women had hard, dull jobs. Their pay was low. Almost all good jobs went to men. After all, people said, a woman's place is in the home. In 1885, the *Pittsburgh Dispatch* printed an **editorial** about working women. It said that women could not do a good job outside the home.

Look Out, World!

Elizabeth Cochrane read the **article**. Elizabeth was born in 1867 in Cochran's Mills, Pennsylvania. In 1885, when she read the article, she was young and eager for adventure. The article made her angry. She wrote to the *Dispatch*. Women, she said, could do many jobs well. It was wrong to waste their talents. The paper printed her letter. Then Cochrane asked for a job as a **reporter.** The **editor** liked her letter. So he gave her a try.

Cochrane wrote under another name. She chose Nellie Bly. "Nellie Bly" is the name of a song by Stephen Foster, an American songwriter who lived in the 1800s.

Travel to Mexico

Nellie Bly's first **reports** told about the hard lives of other working women. She wrote about the slums of Pittsburgh. She wrote about divorce. She got readers excited about her **topics**.

The *Dispatch* saw how popular Bly's work was. So in 1887 the paper sent her to Mexico. For six months, Bly traveled around Mexico. She wrote reports about all that she saw.

In those days, few people saw other countries. There were no movies or TV shows about far-off lands. So almost everything in Bly's reports was new to her readers. They were eager to learn about Mexico. Later, Bly **published** her reports in a book called *Six Months in Mexico*.

Bly Tells All

Soon after Bly came home to Pittsburgh, she moved to New York. She had a new job with a larger paper. She then worked for the *New York World*.

Bly's first big topic in New York was insane asylums. Most often, the city asylums made little news. People with mental illnesses were just "put away" and forgotten. But how well were patients treated? Bly wanted to find out.

Bly knew that visitors are always shown the best things. She wanted to see the worst things too. So she pretended to be insane. She was sent to a New York asylum as a patient.

Inside, Bly learned that patients were often mistreated. Many were dirty and hungry. They were left for long times without care. Instead of getting better, patients got worse.

Two weeks later, Bly was out of the asylum. But the outcome of her daring stunt lasted for years. Her reports about asylums were first printed in the *World*. In 1888, they came out as a book called *Ten Days in a Madhouse*. Readers were shocked by what she wrote. They cried for changes. Because of Bly, life got better for patients in New York asylums.

⬣ **Stop here for the Strategy Break.**

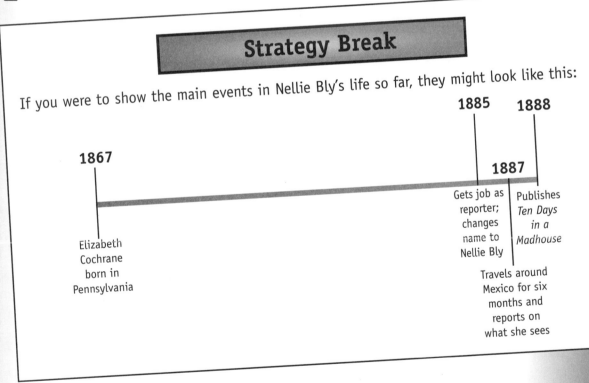

Strategy Break

If you were to show the main events in Nellie Bly's life so far, they might look like this:

1867 — Elizabeth Cochrane born in Pennsylvania

1885 — Gets job as reporter; changes name to Nellie Bly

1887 — Travels around Mexico for six months and reports on what she sees

1888 — Publishes *Ten Days in a Madhouse*

Go on reading.

The Biggest Trip of All

Nellie Bly had proved she was a great reporter. But she still wanted adventure. A book gave her the idea for her greatest success. *Around the World in Eighty Days* was a popular book in 1889. It tells the tale of Phileas Fogg, a noted English gentleman. On a bet, he travels around the world in just 80 days. Few people believed the trip was possible. Bly thought she could make the trip even faster.

At first, the *World* would not let her try. The idea was crazy. No one could go around the world in so few days! And for a woman, there would be added danger. But Bly kept asking. Finally, her boss told her to go ahead. He knew Bly loved adventure. Besides, the trip could make both her and the paper famous.

Bly packed a single bag. Then she set off. On November 14, 1889, at 9:40 A.M., her ship left New Jersey. Bly first landed in England. Then she went on to France. There she met Jules Verne, the writer of *Around the World in Eighty Days*. After Verne wished her good luck, Bly left for Hong Kong.

A Race Against Time

Nellie Bly traveled by ship, train, horse, handcart, and burro. Wherever she went, she wrote. She kept an exact record of what she saw and did. Bly planned to share her adventures with others. She wanted her readers to feel as if they had traveled along with her.

When Bly's ship from Hong Kong reached San Francisco, she was famous. The *World* sent a train to meet her. It would bring her to New Jersey as fast as it could. Even so, crowds met the train at each stop. Everyone wanted to see the young world traveler.

At last, the train reached New Jersey. Bly jumped from it on January 25, 1890, at 3:31 P.M. She had circled Earth in exactly 72 days, 6 hours, and 11 minutes. The waiting crowd cheered. A few days later, New York greeted her. Fireworks went off. Brass bands played. A parade marched down Broadway.

Of course, Bly reported on her trip in the *World*. She also wrote *Nellie Bly's Book: Around the World in Seventy-Two Days* was published in 1890. This was her most popular book.

Other Adventures

Nellie Bly kept up her writing until 1895. Then she married Robert Seaman, a very rich man. After he died, she successfully ran his business. But her gift was for news, not business. By 1920, she was writing again.

Nellie Bly died in 1922. By then, planes carried people over land and seas. Bly's speed record was broken. Yet Bly's boldness is still a model. And her spirit of adventure will never age. ●

Strategy Follow-up

On a wide piece of paper, copy the time line from the Strategy Break. Then continue the time line with dates and information from the second part of this selection.

1889
1890
1895
1920
1922

✓ Personal Checklist

Read each question and put a check (✓) in the correct box.

1. How well do you understand who Elizabeth Cochrane was?
   - ☐ 3 (extremely well)
   - ☐ 2 (fairly well)
   - ☐ 1 (not well)

2. How well were you able to figure out if the boldfaced words were used correctly in the Vocabulary Builder?
   - ☐ 3 (extremely well)
   - ☐ 2 (fairly well)
   - ☐ 1 (not well)

3. How well do you understand why it was remarkable for Nellie Bly to write for a newspaper and travel?
   - ☐ 3 (extremely well)
   - ☐ 2 (fairly well)
   - ☐ 1 (not well)

4. How well do you understand how Nellie Bly's travels and writings helped people?
   - ☐ 3 (extremely well)
   - ☐ 2 (fairly well)
   - ☐ 1 (not well)

5. How well were you able to complete the time line in the Strategy Follow-up?
   - ☐ 3 (extremely well)
   - ☐ 2 (fairly well)
   - ☐ 1 (not well)

Vocabulary Check

Look back at the work you did in the Vocabulary Builder. Then answer each question by circling the correct letter.

1. What does the word *article* mean in the context of this selection?
   a. an item of clothing
   b. a piece of writing
   c. the word *a, an,* or *the*

2. Nellie Bly wrote about many topics. Which phrase defines the word *topics*?
   a. subjects that people write about
   b. creams that people rub on sore body parts
   c. people in insane asylums

3. What does a reporter do?
   a. draw cartoons for a newspaper
   b. writes articles for a newspaper
   c. edits other people's stories

4. Which part of a newspaper is an editorial?
   a. an article that describes a particular news event
   b. an advertisement that helps someone find a job
   c. an article that gives an opinion on a subject

5. What does *report* mean in the context of this selection?
   a. the sound of a shot or an explosion
   b. a rumor or an item of gossip
   c. a written account of something

Add the numbers that you just checked to get your Personal Checklist score. Fill in your score here. Then turn to page 205 and transfer your score onto Graph 1.

Personal		
Vocabulary		
Strategy		
Comprehension		
TOTAL SCORE		
	✓	T

Check your answers with your teacher. Give yourself 1 point for each correct answer, and fill in your Vocabulary score here. Then turn to page 205 and transfer your score onto Graph 1.

Personal		
Vocabulary		
Strategy		
Comprehension		
TOTAL SCORE		
	✓	T

Strategy Check

Review the time line that you completed in the Strategy Follow-up. Then answer these questions:

1. How old was Elizabeth Cochrane when she changed her name to Nellie Bly?
   a. about 18
   b. about 20
   c. about 21

2. What did Bly do in 1888?
   a. left to circle the Earth
   b. married Robert Seaman
   c. published *Ten Days in a Madhouse*

3. When did Bly travel through Mexico?
   a. before she published *Ten Days in a Madhouse*
   b. after she circled the Earth
   c. after she married Robert Seaman

4. For about how long did Bly stop writing?
   a. 10 years
   b. 25 years
   c. 30 years

5. About how old was Nellie Bly when she died?
   a. 28
   b. 53
   c. 55

Comprehension Check

Review the selection if necessary. Then answer these questions:

1. Why was Nellie Bly angry when she read an editorial about women in the *Pittsburgh Dispatch*?
   a. It said that many women had hard, dull jobs.
   b. It said that women should not work outside the home.
   c. It said that women could do many jobs well.

2. What topics did Bly first report on for the *Dispatch*?
   a. slums and divorce
   b. insane asylums and mental illness
   c. all of the above

3. Why did Bly enter a New York insane asylum as a patient?
   a. to learn about the treatment of mentally ill patients
   b. to get better help for mentally ill patients
   c. both of the above

4. Why did Bly want to travel around the world?
   a. to see as many countries as she could
   b. to prove she could do it in under 80 days
   c. to report on different parts of Mexico

5. How did Bly's writings and actions help women?
   a. They proved women could do good work outside the home.
   b. They proved that women could be brave and adventuresome.
   c. Both of the above answers are correct.

Check your answers with your teacher. Give yourself 1 point for each correct answer, and fill in your Strategy score here. Then turn to page 205 and transfer your score onto Graph 1.

Personal
Vocabulary
Strategy
Comprehension
TOTAL SCORE
✓ T

Check your answers with your teacher. Give yourself 1 point for each correct answer, and fill in your Comprehension score here. Then turn to page 205 and transfer your score onto Graph 1.

Personal
Vocabulary
Strategy
Comprehension
TOTAL SCORE
✓ T

Extending

Choose one or more of these activities:

PLAN A TRIP AROUND THE WORLD

Use a world map or a globe to plan a trip around the world. Choose at least six places that you would like to stop. (You might pattern your trip after some of the places that Nellie Bly went. Some of the resources on this page can help, especially the PBS Web site.) Do some research, and write a paragraph telling what you might see on each one of your stops. Include a time line that shows how long you would plan to stay at each stop. Assume this is not a race but an opportunity to see each place.

WRITE A LETTER TO THE EDITOR

Think of a local issue about which you feel strongly. It might be the need to clean up a nearby park, add bike lanes to your neighborhood, or promote a charity. Then write an editorial that you can publish in your class or school newspaper. As another option, read some editorials in your local paper and respond to one of them with your own opinion. Post your letters in the classroom for others to read.

READ THE NEWSPAPER

Read the newspaper, and look for an article written by someone reporting from another country. Make a list of the words and phrases the reporter uses to describe the place. Try to find details that appeal to as many of the five senses as possible (sight, hearing, touch, taste, and sound).

Resources

Books

Around the World in Eighty Days and *Five Weeks in a Balloon* by Jules Verne. Copyright © 1997 by Wordsworth Editions Ltd.

Making Headlines: A Biography of Nellie Bly by Kathy Lynn Emerson. Copyright © 1989 by Dillon Press.

Nellie Bly's Book: Around the World in 72 Days by Nellie Bly and edited by Ira Peck. Copyright © 1999 by Twenty-First Century Books.

Videos

Around the World in 72 Days: The American Experience published by WGBH Boston. (Available through the PBS Web site listed below.)

Around the World in Eighty Days by Jules Verne. Copyright © 1998. ASIN: 6305023565.

Audio Cassette

Around the World in Eighty Days by Jules Verne. Copyright © 1995 by Naxos of America, Inc.

Web Sites

http://www.greatwomen.org/bly.htm
Read about Nellie Bly, and explore this site to learn about other women important to U.S. history.

http://www.pbs.org/wgbh/pages/amex/world/adventure2.html
This PBS site shows a map of the world with each place Nellie Bly stopped on her 72-day tour of the world. Explore the site to learn more about Nellie Bly, or to order the videotape of her life.

Bungee Jumping: A Leap of Faith

The article you are about to read explains why people try bungee jumping. Some of the information will be new to you. But some of it may be information that you have already heard or read. Before you read this article, think of three things that you already know about bungee jumping. Then think of three questions that you have about it. As you read the article, look for answers to your questions.

Vocabulary Builder

1. The words in the margin are all specialized vocabulary words. **Specialized vocabulary** words are related to a particular topic. For example, the words *fungicides, greenhouses, irrigation,* and *pesticides* are all related to growing vegetables.

2. Read the words and phrases below. The words in Column 1 are related to the sport of bungee jumping. Draw a line from each word in Column 1 to its definition in Column 2. Use a dictionary if you need help.

3. Save your work. You will use it again in the Vocabulary Check.

COLUMN 1	COLUMN 2
cords	person who does reckless things for fun
courage	ropes or cables
daredevil	dive
gorge	toy that goes up and down on a string
plunge	long, slender stems of a plant
thrill	excitement
vines	bravery or "guts"
yo-yo	deep, narrow valley

cords

courage

daredevil

gorge

plunge

thrill

vines

yo-yo

Strategy Builder

Outlining Main Ideas and Supporting Details

- As you know, informational articles give facts and details about a particular **topic**. You also know that most informational articles are organized according to **main ideas** and **supporting details**. These ideas and details help explain or support the topic.

- One way to keep track of main ideas and details as you read is to outline them. Some **outlines** use a system of Roman numerals (I, II, III, IV, V, and so on) and capital letters (A, B, C, D, E, and so on).

- Read the following paragraphs, which describe the Big Dipper. Then read the outline of the paragraphs. Note how the main ideas in the paragraphs are identified with Roman numerals, and the supporting details are shown with capital letters.

The Big Dipper

The Big Dipper is part of the constellation called Ursa Major, or the Great Bear. People see many different things when they look at the Big Dipper. Some Native Americans see the bowl of the Big Dipper as a bear. They see the three stars in the handle as three warriors chasing the bear. Other people see the Big Dipper as a cart. Still other people see it as plow, a bull's thigh, and even the Chinese government!

The Big Dipper had an important part in helping Southern slaves escape to freedom. Because the slaves thought that the Big Dipper looked like a ladle for drinking water, they called it the drinking gourd. They used the drinking gourd's North Star to find their way north to Canada.

The Big Dipper

I. The Big Dipper is part of Ursa Major (the Great Bear).

II. People see many different things when they look at the Big Dipper.
   A. Some Native Americans see a bear with three warriors chasing it.
   B. Other people see a cart.
   C. Others see a plow.
   D. Others see a bull's thigh.
   E. Others see the Chinese government.

III. The Big Dipper had an important part in helping slaves escape.
   A. The slaves called the Big Dipper the drinking gourd.
   B. They used its North Star to find their way to Canada.

Bungee Jumping: A Leap of Faith

Look for the main ideas as you read this article. Stop from time to time and think about how you might summarize them.

Bungee jumping began long ago as a ritual on certain islands in the South Pacific. (These islands form the present-day country of Vanuatu.) Each spring the islanders gathered **vines**. They wove them into a kind of rope. Then young men called "land divers" climbed high towers. They tied the vines to their ankles and jumped. They did it to prove their **courage**. A good jump was also supposed to help ensure healthy crops for the island.

Modern bungee jumping began in England on April 1, 1979. Note the day. It was April *Fool's* Day. The members of the Oxford Dangerous Sports Club were looking for a new **thrill**. They had heard of "land diving" and wanted to try it for themselves. So the men climbed up a high bridge, tied rubber **cords** to their ankles, and jumped. One member later said the jump was "quite pleasurable, really."

But it was a man from New Zealand who made bungee jumping a big sport. His name was Alan John Hackett. Hackett was quite a **daredevil**. He had once jumped off the Eiffel Tower in Paris, France. Now, in 1988, he wanted to give others a chance to try bungee jumping. At this time, though, the sport was illegal. So Hackett made a deal with New Zealand police. Using his own money, he would fix up a dilapidated bridge over a river **gorge**. In return, the police let him open a legal bungee jumping center on the bridge.

The center was a huge success. Hackett gave each jumper a special T-shirt. It became a hot item among daredevils. Everyone wanted one of those shirts. And since the only way to get one was to make a jump, more and more people agreed to do it. Some jumpers did really wild things. They asked to jump with an extralong cord. That way they would dip into the river before the cord pulled them back. One man put shampoo on his head. When he bounced up out of the water, he was washing his hair!

 Stop here for the Strategy Break.

Strategy Break

If you were to outline the main ideas and supporting details in this article so far, your outline might look something like this:

Bungee Jumping

I. Bungee jumping began long ago as a ritual in the South Pacific (present-day Vanuatu).
    A. Each spring "land divers" tied vines to their ankles and jumped to prove their courage.
    B. They also did it to ensure healthy crops for the island.
II. Modern bungee jumping began in England on April 1, 1979.
    A. The Oxford Dangerous Sports Club did it for a new thrill.
    B. They tied rubber cords to their ankles and jumped from a high bridge.
III. In 1988 Alan John Hackett of New Zealand made bungee jumping a big sport.
    A. The sport was illegal, but Hackett made a deal with the police to open a legal bungee jumping center.
    B. Everyone wanted one of Hackett's T-shirts, so more and more people signed up to jump.
    C. The jumpers did wild things, such as jumping with extralong cords and putting shampoo in their hair.

As you continue reading, keep paying attention to the main ideas and supporting details. At the end of this article, you will use some of them to create an outline of your own.

 Go on reading.

Bungee jumping soon caught on in the United States. It was introduced in California and Colorado. Then it spread to other states. At first, only the boldest people did it. But over time, others joined in. All kinds of people took the **plunge**. Even one man who was helped out of a wheelchair jumped. And no jumpers complained about paying $50 or more to do it.

As thrills go, it's hard to beat bungee jumping. The platforms used for the jumps are ten stories high—or higher. That means jumpers fall as far as 150 feet before the cord saves them. First-time jumpers can almost taste their fear. Jay Petrow thought about it for a year before he jumped. He said his palms began to sweat just thinking about it. Emily Trask said, "The first time I jumped, I was terrified." Nora Jacobson said, "My terror [was] cold and rippling."

There is, of course, real danger. There is no margin for error in bungee jumping. One mistake, and you're history. And while most people live to tell the tale, a few don't. In 1989 two French jumpers died when their cords broke. A third died when he slammed into a tower. In 1991 Hal Irish became the first American jumper to die. Somehow his cord became detached as he dove through the air.

So accidents *do* happen. But for many, the danger just adds to the excitement. Besides, bungee jumpers don't talk about the tragedies. They talk about the triumphs. They talk about facing their fears. And they talk about the joy of the fall itself. During a jump, a person hits speeds of sixty miles an hour. Then, when the cord tightens, the jumper springs back up into the air like a rocket. For a short time, he or she is a kind of human **yo-yo**, bounding up and down in the breeze. When the cord loses its bounce, the ride is over.

Even then, though, some of the joy remains. Jumpers feel both happy and relieved when it's over. Most laugh and smile as they are unhooked from the cord. "Hey, look at me! I did it!" many of them shout. It is, as one person said, "a natural high." Bungee jumpers even have a name for this soaring feeling. They call it the post-bungee grin. Maybe someday you'll decide to make that leap of faith and share that grin. All it takes is a little money—and a lot of nerve. ●

Strategy Follow-up

Work with a group of classmates to complete this activity. First, review the second part of this article. Then, on a separate sheet of paper, create an outline that begins with "IV. Bungee jumping soon caught on in the United States." Be sure to include only the most important ideas, and skip unnecessary details. If you can, compare your outline with those of other groups. See if your outlines all contain similar information. Revise your group's outline if necessary.

✓Personal Checklist

Read each question and put a check (✓) in the correct box.

1. In Building Background, how well were you able to think of three questions about bungee jumping?
    - ☐ 3   (extremely well)
    - ☐ 2   (fairly well)
    - ☐ 1   (not well)

2. In the Vocabulary Builder, how well were you able to match the specialized vocabulary words and their definitions?
    - ☐ 3   (extremely well)
    - ☐ 2   (fairly well)
    - ☐ 1   (not well)

3. In the Strategy Follow-up, how well were you able to summarize the second part of the article?
    - ☐ 3   (extremely well)
    - ☐ 2   (fairly well)
    - ☐ 1   (not well)

4. How well do you understand the dangers of bungee jumping?
    - ☐ 3   (extremely well)
    - ☐ 2   (fairly well)
    - ☐ 1   (not well)

5. How well do you understand why people bungee jump in spite of the dangers?
    - ☐ 3   (extremely well)
    - ☐ 2   (fairly well)
    - ☐ 1   (not well)

Vocabulary Check

Look back at the work you did in the Vocabulary Builder. Then answer each question by circling the correct letter.

1. Which vocabulary word best describes a personality trait that all bungee jumpers share?
    a. thrill
    b. yo-yo
    c. courage

2. Which vocabulary word describes a person who does reckless things for the thrill of it?
    a. yo-yo
    b. daredevil
    b. gorge

3. Alan Hackett set up his bunging jumping center on a bridge over a river gorge. Which phrase describes a gorge?
    a. mountain with water running down it
    b. deep valley with water running through it
    c. dry, flat land with water running through

4. Why does the article compare bungee jumpers to human yo-yos?
    a. because they both bounce up and down from a cord
    b. because they both fly in and out from a cord
    c. because they both spin in circles as they bounce

5. Which vocabulary word best describes the action of a jumper as he or she dives off a platform or bridge?
    a. courage
    b. plunge
    c. thrill

Add the numbers that you just checked to get your Personal Checklist score. Fill in your score here. Then turn to page 205 and transfer your score onto Graph 1.

	Personal	
	Vocabulary	
	Strategy	
	Comprehension	
TOTAL SCORE		
	✓	T

Check your answers with your teacher. Give yourself 1 point for each correct answer, and fill in your Vocabulary score here. Then turn to page 205 and transfer your score onto Graph 1.

	Personal	
	Vocabulary	
	Strategy	
	Comprehension	
TOTAL SCORE		
	✓	T

Strategy Check

Look back at your summary for the second part of this article. Then answer these questions:

1. Which sentence does not summarize one of this article's main ideas?
   a. At first, only the boldest people did it.
   b. As thrills go, it's hard to beat bungee jumping.
   c. Bungee jumping accidents *do* happen.

2. Which sentence *does* summarize one of this article's main ideas?
   a. Hal Irish became the first American jumper to die.
   b. Most laugh and smile as they are unhooked from the cord.
   c. As thrills go, it's hard to beat bungee jumping.

3. Which phrase best states the topic of this article?
   a. bungee jumping
   b. bungee accidents
   c. bungee jumpers

4. Name one of the dangers of bungee jumping that this article describes.
   a. bouncing like a yo-yo
   b. having the cord break
   c. having the cord tighten

5. Which sentence best summarizes this entire article?
   a. Bungee jumping began long ago as a ritual.
   b. First-time jumpers can almost taste their fear.
   c. Bungee jumping is a real leap of faith.

Comprehension Check

Review the article if necessary. Then answer these questions:

1. Where did the earliest bungee jumping take place?
   a. in England
   b. in California
   c. in the South Pacific

2. Why did modern bungee jumping begin?
   a. A sports club was looking for a new thrill.
   b. Some islanders wanted to ensure healthy crops.
   c. A man wanted to bungee jump off the Eiffel Tower.

3. During a jump, what speed can a bungee jumper reach?
   a. six miles an hour
   b. sixteen miles an hour
   c. sixty miles an hour

4. How did the first American bungee jumper die?
   a. He slammed into a tower.
   b. His cord became detached.
   c. His cord broke.

5. Which quote sums up why some people bungee jump?
   a. It was "quite pleasurable, really."
   b. "Hey, look at me! I did it!"
   c. Both of the above answers are correct.

Check your answers with your teacher. Give yourself 1 point for each correct answer, and fill in your Strategy score here. Then turn to page 205 and transfer your score onto Graph 1.

Personal	
Vocabulary	
Strategy	
Comprehension	
TOTAL SCORE	✓ T

Check your answers with your teacher. Give yourself 1 point for each correct answer, and fill in your Comprehension score here. Then turn to page 205 and transfer your score onto Graph 1.

Personal	
Vocabulary	
Strategy	
Comprehension	
TOTAL SCORE	✓ T

Extending

Choose one or both of these activities:

MAKE A CATALOG

Make a short catalog of some of the equipment necessary for safe bungee jumping. The Web sites listed on this page will give you a place to start. Or you can talk to someone at your local sporting goods store. Include your own drawing or a photo with the description of each item. Tell what the item is for and how it is used.

MAKE "STAT SHEETS"

Research the most popular bungee jumping locations in the world. Then write a "stat sheet" for each location that includes the following information:

- the country, state, and/or town in which the jump is located
- its height in both feet and meters
- how many people have made the jump from that location
- the most unusual jump or jumps made from that location

Resources

Book

Bungee Jumping by Jim Glaser. Copyright © 1999 by Capstone Press.

Web Sites

http://bungeeamerica.com/
This is the official Web site of Bungee America, founded in 1989 in California. The site includes information on equipment and training.

http://www.bigeventcompany.com/bungee.htm
This site gives schedules for a traveling bungee structure. See if it will be visiting a location near you!

LESSON 10
Too-Tall Twyla

Building Background

Have you ever played or watched a basketball game? What words did you use or hear? Think about all of the **specialized vocabulary words** that people use during basketball games, such as *dribble, rebound,* and *fast break.* Add the words to the concept map (web) below. As you read "Too-Tall Twyla" look for more basketball words to add to your web. When you finish reading the story, compare your web with a classmate.

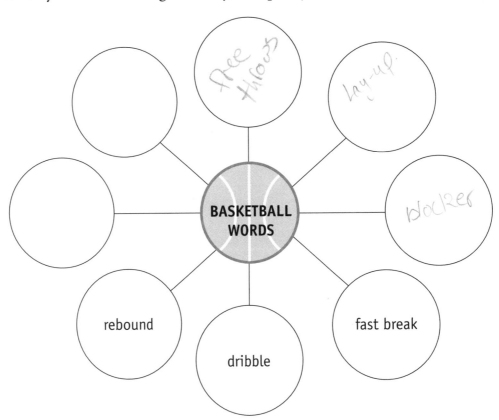

coed

forfeit

routines

nickname

MVP

hesitate

accurate

stunned

Vocabulary Builder

1. Read the vocabulary words in the margin, and think about what they mean. Then read the sentences below. On each line, write the vocabulary word in parentheses that best fits the sentence. As you read the story, you may decide to change some of your answers.

   a. If your team has to quit a game before finishing, you must

   _____ the game. (forfeit, routine)

   b. The _____ of a game is usually the one

   who played the best. (nickname, MVP)

c. If your ball goes through the hoop every time you shoot, you

are _____ . (hesitate, accurate)

d. A team that has a mix of female and male players is a

_____ team. (coed, stunned)

2. On a separate sheet of paper, write a sentence for each word that you didn't circle. Use story context to help you, or look up the words in a dictionary.

3. Save your work. You will use it again in the Vocabulary Check.

Strategy Builder

Making Predictions While Reading a Story

- While you read, you often make predictions. A **prediction** is a kind of guess. To make a prediction, act like a detective. Use the story's most important information, or clues, to figure out what might happen next.

- The clues in a story are sometimes called context clues. **Context** is the information that comes before or after a word or situation to help you understand it better. In this story some of the context clues are basketball terms. If you don't know a lot about basketball, you might ask a classmate to explain some of the terms.

- As you read "Too-Tall Twyla," you will stop twice to make predictions. At each Strategy Break, you will be asked to write down which context clues helped you make your predictions. Then, after you finish reading the story, you will look back at your predictions and check your work.

Too-Tall Twyla

by Russell Lewis

See if you can use clues that the author provides to help you make predictions while you read.

Shawn and Terry caught the flu, Roland broke his leg, and Jared moved away. Suddenly our Midcity boys' basketball team was down to five players and zero substitutes.

Coach Allens talked to us after school. "League rules require at least one player on the bench. We have two choices. One, we can **forfeit** the championship game with Central this Friday."

"Forfeit? No way!" I exclaimed. "They only beat us by two points last year. This is *our* year to win!"

"Can't we just suit up some kid—any kid?" Mark asked.

Mark was our superstar, the reason we knew this was our year to finally beat Central. He never missed when he had an open shot. He was the league's best shot blocker and rebounder, too. The only time our subs got on the court was when Coach wanted to give Mark a breather!

Well, league rules or not, Coach wasn't about to suit up just any kid. "What if one of our players gets hurt?" he asked. "That sub would have to go into the game, right?"

We all nodded.

"So we need the best player we can get, right?"

We all nodded again.

"So choice number two is..." Coach paused. "The league office said Twyla could play for us."

"Too-Tall Twyla?" everyone exclaimed.

Twyla was my big sister. She was also captain of our girls' basketball team. Twyla had loved to play basketball ever since fourth grade, when she suddenly shot up six inches taller than any boy in the class. That's when she got the nickname "Too-Tall."

She was a pretty good player, too. So when we thought about our choices—either forfeit the game or let Twyla sit on the bench—we didn't **hesitate**. We became the first **coed** basketball team in Midcity's history!

We had one more practice before the big game. Coach had us practice our fast breaks, passing the ball back and forth as we raced down the court.

"Hey, Sis," I yelled. "Don't try to shoot every time you get the ball. Pass the ball to me!"

"But I was open," Twyla yelled back. "Didn't Coach say to shoot if you had an open shot?" Her shot had just swished through the hoop, touching nothing but net.

"Yeah, but he also said to pass the ball around, be a team player!" I was kind of embarrassed. *My* shot had just bounced off the rim, missing badly. Oh well, I thought. It'll be Mark, not Twyla, in the real game.

The real game for the league championship was tomorrow against Central. This was going to be our year, we thought—especially with Mark playing as well as he was.

On Friday the whole school was buzzing. At lunchtime the cheerleaders did their **routines** in the cafeteria. They made each of us players stand up as we were introduced. When Mark's name was called, the whole place went bonkers. Mark was our superstar, and all the kids knew it!

 Stop here for Strategy Break #1.

Strategy Break #1

Use the information in the story to help you answer these questions:

1. What do you predict will happen next?

_____

_____

2. Why do you think so?

_____

_____

3. What clues from the story helped you make your prediction(s)?

_____

_____

 Go on reading to see what happens.

After school everyone crowded into the gymnasium. When we ran onto the court to begin our warm-up drills, the cheerleaders jumped up and down, waving their pompons. My heart began pumping like a jackhammer, my mouth felt as if it were stuffed with cotton, and my knees were shaking so hard I thought they would buckle.

After we ran through a few drills, I began to feel a little more normal. Then the warning buzzer sounded, and Coach called us over for a meeting.

"Remember what you've learned," he said as we huddled around him. "Teamwork—passing—look for the open player. If they double-team Mark, that means someone else is open."

We broke out of the huddle with a shout. I was still nervous. It was a good feeling, though, being all pumped up for the game. I knew that this year we were going to win!

We jumped off to an early six-point lead, then held our own until halftime. Mark shot 80 percent from the floor and had five rebounds. No one on Central's team could even come close to matching up with him.

They must have talked it over during halftime. When the second half started, they had two players guarding Mark. That stopped us for a little while, but not for long.

"Look for the open player!" someone yelled from our bench. It was Twyla. She was standing on the sidelines screaming at us as we raced down the court. "You can do it!" she yelled. "Yea, Midcity! Yea, team!"

I had to admit she was right. Every time they put two defenders on Mark, one of us was always left open. But our shooting wasn't as **accurate** as Mark's. Central slowly crept back to within one basket of tying the game.

Then disaster struck. Cutting between two Central players, Mark tripped and fell. The referees stopped play when they saw him rolling on the floor in pain, holding his left ankle.

"It's a bad sprain," Coach announced. "Mark's out for the rest of the game." His face was grim as he turned to Twyla. "Report to the scoring table, Twyla. You're going in for Mark."

Twyla looked scared. She looked at Coach with a frozen expression on her face.

I knew just how she felt. I remembered my jackhammer heart, my cottony mouth, my shaking knees. "You'll do O.K., Twyla," I said. "Just remember what Coach says. Look for the open man . . . er, uh, person!"

Everyone laughed at that. Even Twyla. Then the buzzer sounded, and we took our places on the floor again.

 Stop here for Strategy Break #2.

Strategy Break #2

Use the information in the story to help you answer these questions:
1. Do your earlier predictions match what happened? _____ Why or why not?

_____

_____

2. What do you predict will happen next?

_____

_____

3. Why do you think so?

_____

_____

4. What clues from the story helped you make your prediction(s)?

_____

_____

 Go on reading to see what happens.

"Look what we've got!" shouted the Central players. "The Midcity *girls'* team!" They cracked up laughing. They thought the game was all wrapped up now.

That's the way it looked to me, too. Twyla was scared stiff and not playing well. It was as if we only had four players instead of five. The Central team didn't even bother guarding her. They put the extra player on whichever one of us had the ball.

With three minutes to go, the score was tied. Soon we were down by one basket, then by two. By the time Central pulled into a ten-point lead, we began to play as if we had just about given up.

Even when Sis blocked a shot, we didn't really pay much attention. After all, her **nickname** wasn't "Too-Tall" for nothing! But the next time she blocked a shot, she rebounded the ball herself, dribbled the length of the floor, and sank an easy lay-up.

That got everyone's attention. It jarred Twyla out of her frozen state, too. She blocked shot after shot, rebounded at both ends of the court, and passed the ball to the open player on our fast breaks. She swished nearly every one of her own shots.

The Central team was **stunned** and confused. They weren't laughing now.

Then, with the score tied and only seconds left on the clock, Twyla blocked another Central shot. Expecting another fast break, I started to run up the floor.

"Double-team her!" someone on their team shouted. Two Central players trapped Twyla in the corner.

Twisting her head left and right, she spotted me in the lane, wide open. With a quick head fake, Twyla drew one of the Central players out of position, then pushed a two-handed bounce pass to me under his outstretched arms.

I took the pass, made an easy lay-up as the buzzer sounded—and it was all over.

Final score—Midcity 48, Central 46. We had won! We were the new league champions!

We hugged and laughed and slapped high-fives. Mark had a big grin on his face. So did Coach. Everyone was slapping Twyla on the back. She was grinning, too.

"We're a girl's team, all right," Mark said, "and her name is Twyla! But 'Too-Tall' isn't the right nickname for our **MVP**."

I laughed. "I know her new nickname. It's what Central's probably calling her right now—'Too-Much' Twyla!" ●

Strategy Follow-up

Go back and look at the predictions that you wrote in this lesson. Do any of them match what actually happened in the story? Why or why not?

✓Personal Checklist

Read each question and put a check (✓) in the correct box.

1. How well were you able to understand the basketball terms in this story?
   - ☐ 3 (extremely well)
   - ☐ 2 (fairly well)
   - ☐ 1 (not well)

2. In the Vocabulary Builder, how many words were you able to use correctly in sentences?
   - ☐ 3 (6–8 words)
   - ☐ 2 (3–5 words)
   - ☐ 1 (0–2 words)

3. How well were you able to use context clues to predict what would happen next in this story?
   - ☐ 3 (extremely well)
   - ☐ 2 (fairly well)
   - ☐ 1 (not well)

4. How well do you understand why Twyla was chosen to play on the team?
   - ☐ 3 (extremely well)
   - ☐ 2 (fairly well)
   - ☐ 1 (not well)

5. How well do you understand why no one guarded Twyla when she first began to play?
   - ☐ 3 (extremely well)
   - ☐ 2 (fairly well)
   - ☐ 1 (not well)

Vocabulary Check

Look back at the work you did in the Vocabulary Builder. Then answer each question by circling the correct letter.

1. Why does Mark call Twyla the MVP of the game?
   a. because she came in off the bench and played
   b. because she did the most to help the team win
   c. because she was a girl on a boys' team

2. What does the word *hesitate* mean?
   a. wait
   b. move
   c. decide

3. Why was Central's team stunned during the game?
   a. They didn't expect Mark to hurt himself.
   b. They didn't expect Twyla to play as she did.
   c. They didn't expect to win the game.

4. Which of the following is not a routine?
   a. eating a donut after school every day
   b. giving one person a special nickname
   c. practicing lay-ups and free throws

5. The narrator says that his team's shooting isn't as accurate as Mark's. What is another word for *accurate*?
   a. poor
   b. imperfect
   c. exact

Add the numbers that you just checked to get your Personal Checklist score. Fill in your score here. Then turn to page 205 and transfer your score onto Graph 1.

	Personal	
Personal		
Vocabulary		
Strategy		
Comprehension		
TOTAL SCORE		
	✓	T

Check your answers with your teacher. Give yourself 1 point for each correct answer, and fill in your Vocabulary score here. Then turn to page 205 and transfer your score onto Graph 1.

	Personal	
Personal		
Vocabulary		
Strategy		
Comprehension		
TOTAL SCORE		
	✓	T

Strategy Check

Look back at what you wrote at each Strategy Break. Then answer these questions:

1. At Strategy Break #1, if you had predicted that Twyla's team would win the game, which clue would have best supported your prediction?

    a. Shawn and Terry caught the flu.

    b. "This is our year to win."

    c. "Too-Tall Twyla?" everyone exclaimed.

2. If you had predicted that Twyla would have to join the game, which clue would have best supported your prediction?

    a. "What if one of our players gets hurt?"

    b. Twyla was my big sister.

    c. "Too-Tall Twyla?" everyone exclaimed.

3. At Strategy Break #2, which prediction would not have fit this story?

    a. Twyla will get hurt too.

    b. Twyla will play for the other team.

    c. Twyla will make many baskets.

4. At Strategy Break #2, if you had predicted that the narrator's team would win, which clue would have best supported your prediction?

    a. She was a pretty good player, too.

    b. Mark was our superstar.

    c. Twyla look scared.

5. Which clue helped you know that Twyla was a good basketball player?

    a. She had a nickname.

    b. She loved to play basketball.

    c. Her shots didn't even touch the net.

Comprehension Check

Review the story if necessary. Then answer these questions:

1. Why is this game so important to both teams?

    a. It is the league championship.

    b. It is the first game of the year.

    c. It is the first game Twyla will play.

2. Why is it so unusual for Twyla to play on this team?

    a. Mark never got hurt before.

    b. Twyla was a girl on a boys' team.

    c. Twyla never passed the ball.

3. Why does Twyla have to play in the second half?

    a. Mark fouls out of the game.

    b. Mark is tired and leaves the game.

    c. Mark gets hurt and leaves the game.

4. What happens to make Twyla and her team start playing better?

    a. Mark gets hurt.

    b. Twyla makes a lay-up.

    c. The buzzer sounds.

5. Why might Central call Twyla "Too-Much Twyla?"

    a. because she has so much skill

    b. because she doesn't pass the ball enough

    c. because she is gaining weight

Check your answers with your teacher. Give yourself 1 point for each correct answer, and fill in your Strategy score here. Then turn to page 205 and transfer your score onto Graph 1.

Personal	
Vocabulary	
Strategy	
Comprehension	
TOTAL SCORE	.
✓ T	

Check your answers with your teacher. Give yourself 1 point for each correct answer, and fill in your Comprehension score here. Then turn to page 205 and transfer your score onto Graph 1.

Personal	
Vocabulary	
Strategy	
Comprehension	
TOTAL SCORE	
✓ T	

Extending

Choose one or both of these activities:

MAKE BASKETBALL CARDS OR POSTERS

Make basketball cards or posters for your school's or league's team. Include a picture of each player, information about the position he or she plays, average points scored per game, and other important statistics. Use the resources listed on this page for ideas about what to include. Display the cards during every game.

CREATE "PLAYERS WANTED" POSTERS

Learn about the Women's National Basketball League and what it takes to become a player. Create a "wanted" poster for a particular WNBA team. Include all the requirements and personal characteristics that a player would need for this league. You can use one of the resources listed on this page for ideas and information.

Resources

Books

Basketball by Dennis Tuttle. Copyright © 1999 by Chelsea House Publishers.

We Got Next! by Gail Herman. Copyright © 1998 by Putnam Publishing Group.

Collecting Basketball Cards by Thomas Owens. Copyright © 1998 by Millbrook Press, Inc.

You Can Be a Woman Basketball Player by Tamecka Dixon and Judith Cohen. Copyright © 1999 by Cascade Pass, Inc.

Alonzo Mourning with contributions by Chuck Daly. Copyright © 1999 by Chelsea House Publishers.

Web Sites

http://www.washingtonpost.com/wp-srv/sports/mystics.htm
Here is the place to get up-to-the-minute information on the Mystics, a WNBA team.

http://www.wnba.com/monarchs/index.html
Information on the Sacramento Monarchs, another WNBA team, is provided on this Web site.

Videos

Teaching Kids Basketball with John Wooden by ESPN. Subtitles in English. ASIN: 6301718313.

Let's Play Basketball. Copyright © 1995 by ESPN. ASIN: 6303312179.

Basketball for Woman Defense. Copyright © 1998. Starring N. Lieberman-Cline. ASIN: 6305240590.

60 Minute Basketball Skills Workout. ASIN: 6303121888.

Game Smart: How to Watch Basketball. Copyright © 1995. Starring Lute Olson. ASIN: 6304618107.

Learning New Words

Compound Words

VOCABULARY

From Lesson 9
• daredevil

A compound word is made up of two words put together. In Lesson 9 you read about daredevil bungee jumpers. *Daredevil* is made of the words *dare* and *devil*. *Daredevil* is a name given to a person who does recklessly daring things for fun and thrills.

Fill in each blank with a compound word by combining a word from Row 1 with a word from Row 2.

Row 1:   suit   cook   tear   table   wrist

Row 2:   ware   cloth   watch   jerker   case

1. very sad movie or book = _____

2. bag used to hold things while traveling = _____

3. clock that's worn on the arm = _____

4. pots and pans = _____

5. covering for an eating surface = _____

Suffixes

From Lesson 8
• reporter

A suffix is a word part that is added to the end of a root word. When you add a suffix, you often change the root word's meaning and function. For example, the suffix *-ful* means "full of," so the root word *pain* changes from a noun to an adjective meaning "full of pain."

-er

The suffix *-er* is a special kind of suffix. It turns a verb into a noun that means "a person who _____." In Nellie Bly's biography you learned that a *reporter* is a person who writes reports, or articles, for a newspaper.

Write the word that describes each person below.

1. a person who builds houses   _____

2. a person who writes books   _____

3. a person who leads others   _____

4. a person who designs things   _____

-or

The suffix *-or* does the same thing as *-er:* It turns a verb into a noun that means "a person who ____." Besides learning about reporters in Nellie Bly's biography, you learned about editors. In that selection, the *editor* was the person who ran the newspaper. However, an editor also can be a person who edits articles or books.

Write a description for each person below.

1. decorator _____

2. sculptor _____

3. actor _____

4. creator _____

5. visitor _____

-ist

The suffix *-ist* has a similar function to *-er* and *-or.* It, too, turns words into nouns that mean "a person who ____." For example, in Lesson 7 you learned that Marian Anderson's *accompanist* was the person who accompanied her, or played the piano with her, while she sang.

Now write the word that describes each person below.

1. a person who plays the piano _____

2. a person who makes or performs art _____

3. a person who tours a place _____

4. a person who's an expert in chemistry _____

5. a person who terrorizes others _____

VOCABULARY

From Lesson 8
• editor

From Lesson 7
• accompanist

Dava's Talent

Building Background

"Dava's Talent" is a story set in Morocco, a country in the northwestern tip of Africa, where raising sheep has always been a way of life. People who work in the deserts of Morocco often wear long-sleeved, hooded robes called djellabahs (jə lä′ bə). Djellabahs help protect people from the scorching sun and drifting sand.

bleat

flock

herd

lambs

sheared

sheepcote

shepherd

Vocabulary Builder

1. The words in the margin are all related to sheep and their care. Read the words and see if you recognize any of them.

2. Before you read "Dava's Talent," try to match as many of the words in Column 1 to their definitions in Column 2 by drawing lines between them.

3. Then, as you read, find the rest of the words in context and try to figure out their meanings. Match the rest of the words, and change any of your earlier matches.

4. Save your work. You will use it again in the Vocabulary Check.

COLUMN 1	COLUMN 2
sheared	baby sheep
shepherd	cut the wool from a sheep
herd	group of sheep
sheepcote	person who cares for sheep
bleat	small fenced yard where sheep are kept
flock	sound a sheep makes
lambs	move sheep as a group

Strategy Builder

Identifying Cause-and-Effect Relationships in Stories

- Stories are often built on a framework of **cause-and-effect relationships**, similar to real life. For example, picture yourself asleep in bed, happily dreaming away. You hear a loud buzz as your alarm goes off (cause), and you wake up (effect). If you were to ask yourself, "What happened?" you would realize that you woke up. If you asked, "Why did it happen?" the answer would be "because the alarm sounded."

- Pay attention to the causes and effects as you read the following paragraph.

Mighty Pup is my favorite puppy in the litter. But he's not my mom's favorite. One day he was bouncing around so much that he knocked over his water bowl. That got the floor *and* his paws all wet. Next he put his wet paws in the food bowl and then bounded around the room. He made paw marks all over the furniture! All of Mighty Pup's noise caused Mom to come into the room. When she saw what he had done, she exclaimed, "Oh no! That's a Mighty *Messy* Pup!"

- If you wanted to track the causes and effects in the paragraph, you could put them on a **cause-and-effect chain**. It might look like this:

CAUSES

Mighty Pup knocks over his water bowl.

He puts his wet paws in the food bowl and bounds around the room.

Mom hears the noise and comes into the room.

EFFECTS

That gets the floor and his paws all wet.

He makes paw marks all over the furniture.

She says he's a Mighty Messy Pup.

Dava's Talent

by Lee Ebler

As you read the first part of this story, you can apply the strategies that you just learned. To find the causes and effects, keep asking yourself, "What happened?" and "Why did it happen?"

Dava loved sheep. He loved their cries and their thick coats. He loved to play with the **lambs** and he especially loved to fill the woolsack when Papa **sheared**. Dava's papa was a **shepherd**, and his family lived near a river and mountains in a small village in Morocco.

Dava thought sheep were wonderful, but he could not **herd** them very well. When he wanted them to go right, they went left. When he wanted them to go uphill, they went downhill. And when he wanted them to drink, they stood in the brook and splashed while Dava got wet and sneezy.

"All your forefathers have been shepherds," said Uncle Eban. "Why won't the sheep obey you?"

"I don't know," said Dava sadly.

"Maybe if you wear Papa's clothes," suggested his sister Leah, "the sheep will think you're Papa and mind you."

So Dava put on Papa's djellabah. The sleeves covered his hands, and the hem dragged on the ground. When he walked toward the sheep, he tripped and fell. The sheep were not fooled. While Dava struggled out of the djellabah, they got into the garden and ate the melons.

"Perhaps you should walk slower when you lead the sheep," said Mama. "Sheep do not like bouncy shepherds."

So Dava walked slowly. But he was so slow that the sheep thought he was a tree. They chewed on his sash, leaving it sticky and shredded. Dava decided that walking slowly wasn't the answer.

"Every shepherd has a talent to offer," said Papa. "When you find yours, the sheep will obey. Uncle Eban plays the flute. My talent is singing. We both lead the herd with our music."

"Maybe I'm a singer like Papa," said Dava to Bright Eyes, the smallest sheep. He began to sing in a loud voice about streams and green grass. He thought he had found his talent until Leah chased him away from the house.

"Your music sounds like rocks falling!" she said, slamming the door.

"I will loan you my flute," said Uncle Eban. "It's clear that you are not a singer."

So Dava played the flute. He practiced inside the **sheepcote** until Uncle Eban stuck wool in his ears and the sheep began to **bleat**. They did not like his flute playing.

"You screech like a hawk!" said Uncle Eban, taking back the flute. "You're scaring the sheep."

"I will never be a good shepherd," said Dava to Bright Eyes.

⬡ **Stop here for the Strategy Break.**

Strategy Break

If you were to create a cause-and-effect chain for this story so far, it might look like this:

CAUSES   **EFFECTS**

| Dava puts on his Papa's djellabah. | The sheep are not fooled. They go into the garden and eat the melons. |

| Dava walks more slowly. | The sheep think he is a tree and chew on his sash. |

| Dava sings in a loud voice. | Leah chases him away and says his music sounds like rocks falling. |

| Dava plays Uncle Eban's flute. | He scares the sheep, and they begin to bleat. |

 Go on reading to see what happens.

One day a terrible thing happened. Papa and Uncle Eban were repairing the stone wall. They were working fast because a storm was coming. Suddenly one of the rocks fell on Papa's foot. Dava could see that it hurt. He started toward Papa, but Uncle Eban stopped him.

"I'll take your papa home, but you must lead the sheep back by yourself. Take them slowly, as you have learned."

"But I can't," said Dava. "The sheep won't listen to me."

"Please try," said Uncle Eban.

Dava watched Papa and Uncle Eban leave. The sky was getting dark, and the wind was rising. The sheep began to bleat.

Dava picked up the staff and swished it around. "Hoy!" he shouted. "Hoy, Trud and Bright Eyes. Hoy, Spots!"

But the sheep did not listen. Thunder echoed over the mountains, and the frightened sheep moved toward the broken wall. If Dava didn't stop them, they would run into the desert.

Almost without thinking, Dava began to whistle softly. The sheep didn't hear it, but the whistle calmed Dava. So he whistled louder. Beside him, Bright Eyes stopped trembling.

Then Dava had an idea. He stood in the center of the herd and whistled. He whistled a hopeful tune, a cheerful tune, an everything's-all-right tune. And the sheep understood. They grew calm, because Dava was calm. Still whistling, Dava led them toward the sheepcote. He knew the sheep trusted him now. He felt as if he were part of the **flock**.

I am a whistler, thought Dava, smiling.

The sheep came safely home that day, and Papa was soon feeling well enough to hear Dava's story. ●

Strategy Follow-up

Complete this cause-and-effect chain for the second part of the story. Copy it onto another sheet of paper if you need more room to write.

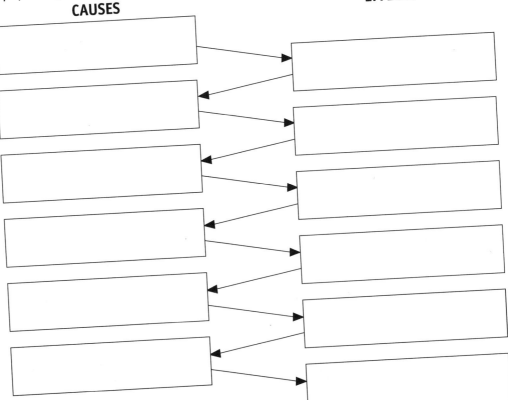

✓Personal Checklist

Read each question and put a check (✓) in the correct box.

1. How well do you understand why people wear djellabahs in Morocco?
   - ☐ 3 (extremely well)
   - ☐ 2 (fairly well)
   - ☐ 1 (not well)

2. How well were you able to match the words and definitions in the Vocabulary Builder?
   - ☐ 3 (extremely well)
   - ☐ 2 (fairly well)
   - ☐ 1 (not well)

3. How well do you understand why Dava has trouble getting the sheep to follow him?
   - ☐ 3 (extremely well)
   - ☐ 2 (fairly well)
   - ☐ 1 (not well)

4. How well do you understand why the sheep are in danger when the wall is broken?
   - ☐ 3 (extremely well)
   - ☐ 2 (fairly well)
   - ☐ 1 (not well)

5. How well were you able to complete the cause-and-effect chain in the Strategy Follow-up?
   - ☐ 3 (extremely well)
   - ☐ 2 (fairly well)
   - ☐ 1 (not well)

Vocabulary Check

Look back at the work you did in the Vocabulary Builder. Then answer each question by circling the correct letter.

1. What is a sheepcote?
   - a. a small fenced yard where sheep are kept
   - b a robe that protects from the sun and sand
   - c. a tool that is used to cut off a sheep's coat

2. What do you call a group of sheep?
   - a. a bleat
   - b. a flock
   - c. a sheepcote

3. What is most similar to a sheep being sheared?
   - a. a person getting a haircut
   - b. a person having an operation
   - c. a dog walking on a leash

4. What might someone herd besides sheep?
   - a. birds
   - b. cats
   - c. cattle

5. What are baby sheep called?
   - a. sheep
   - b. flocks
   - c. lambs

Add the numbers that you just checked to get your Personal Checklist score. Fill in your score here. Then turn to page 205 and transfer your score onto Graph 1.

Personal	
Vocabulary	
Strategy	
Comprehension	
TOTAL SCORE	
	✓ T

Check your answers with your teacher. Give yourself 1 point for each correct answer, and fill in your Vocabulary score here. Then turn to page 205 and transfer your score onto Graph 1.

Personal	
Vocabulary	
Strategy	
Comprehension	
TOTAL SCORE	
	✓ T

Strategy Check

Look back at the cause-and-effect chain that you completed in the Strategy Follow-up. Then answer these questions:

1. What effect does Dava's father's injury have?
   a. The sheep follow Dava's father to the wall.
   b. Dava must lead the sheep back by himself.
   c. The sheep understand and grow calm.

2. Dava swishes the staff around and calls to the sheep. What effect does this have on them?
   a. The sheep do not listen and move toward the wall.
   b. The sheep grow very frightened.
   c. The sheep understand and grow calm.

3. What causes Bright Eyes to stop trembling?
   a. A rock falls on Papa's foot.
   b. Dava calls to the sheep.
   c. Dava begins to whistle louder.

4. What is the effect when Dava begins to whistle softly?
   a. The sheep begin bleating very loudly.
   b. The sheep don't hear it, but it calms Dava.
   c. The sheep begin moving toward the wall.

5. What causes Dava to realize he is a whistler?
   a. His whistling calmed down the sheep.
   b. His whistling led the sheep safely home.
   c. Both of the above answers are correct.

Comprehension Check

Review the story if necessary. Then answer these questions:

1. What is Dava's problem at the beginning of the story?
   a. Dava thinks sheep are awful, but he must herd them all the time.
   b. Dava thinks sheep are wonderful, but he can't herd them very well.
   c. Dava thinks sheep are wonderful, and they go just where he wants them to.

2. Why does Dava wear his father's djellabah?
   a. so the sheep will think Dava is his father and will listen to him
   b. so the sheep will think Dava is funny and will listen to him
   c. so the sheep will be afraid of Dava and will listen to him

3. Why does Dava sing to the sheep?
   a. He loves to sing, and he wants to entertain the sheep.
   b. Leah and Uncle Eban ask Dava to sing them a song.
   c. He's trying to find his talent so the sheep will obey him.

4. What makes Dava feel as if he is part of the flock?
   a. He can bleat just like the sheep can.
   b. He knows the sheep trust him now.
   c. Both of the above answers are correct.

5. What does Dava's talent turn out to be?
   a. whistling
   b. singing
   c. shouting

Check your answers with your teacher. Give yourself 1 point for each correct answer, and fill in your Strategy score here. Then turn to page 205 and transfer your score onto Graph 1.

	Personal	
	Vocabulary	
	Strategy	
	Comprehension	
TOTAL SCORE		
	✓ T	

Check your answers with your teacher. Give yourself 1 point for each correct answer, and fill in your Comprehension score here. Then turn to page 205 and transfer your score onto Graph 1.

	Personal	
	Vocabulary	
	Strategy	
	Comprehension	
TOTAL SCORE		
	✓ T	

Extending

Choose one or both of these activities:

LEARN ABOUT MOROCCO

Work with a small group of classmates to find information about Morocco. Use the resources listed on this page or ones that you find yourselves. Divide up the following topics, and share your findings in an oral or written report: history, government, agriculture, land and climate, people, customs, foods.

HOLD A CONTEST

Here's a contest for you to try: Form teams of three or four students each. Have a referee set a timer for a certain amount of time. When the referee says, "Go," brainstorm a list of stories or songs in which a shepherd, a sheep, or a lamb plays a role. When the referee says, "Stop," compare lists. Which team has the most stories or songs? How many stories or songs did both teams list? If you'd like, repeat the same procedure with stories or songs that have to do with whistling or singing.

Resources

Books

Children of Morocco by Jules Harmes. Copyright © 1995 by Carolrhoda Books.

Morocco by Ettagale Blauer and Jason Laure. Copyright © 1999 by Children's Press.

Morocco by Pat Seward. Copyright © 1995 by Marshall Cavendish Corporation.

Morocco by NTC Publishing Group Staff. Copyright © 1998 by NTC/Contemporary Publishing Company.

Morocco in Pictures edited by Lerner Publications Geography Staff. Copyright © 1996 by Lerner Publishing Group.

LESSON 12

Feeling Sleepy?

Building Background

How much sleep do you usually get each night? People need different amounts of sleep at different ages. Study the chart and answer the questions below it to decide if you get enough sleep.

Age	Actual Hours of Sleep*	Hours of Sleep Needed**
9 and under	9 ¼	10 ¼
10–11	9	9 ¾
12	8 ¼	9 ¼
13 and older	7 ¾	9

* Source: *Zillions* Opinion Poll, January/February 1998.
** Source: The Center for Pediatric Sleep Disorders at Boston Children's Hospital.

1. What time do you usually go to bed? _____

2. What time do you usually wake up? _____

3. How much sleep do you usually get each night? _____

4. According to the chart, how much sleep *should* you be getting?

   _____

5. At what age will your sleep requirements change? _____

Vocabulary Builder

1. The words in Column 1 on page 115 are from "Feeling Sleepy?" They are all related to sleep and its effects on the body.

2. Draw a line from each word in Column 1 to its definition in Column 2. If you're not sure of any of the words, guess for now. Then come back and check or change your answers as you find the boldfaced terms in the article.

catnaps

functions

internal "clock"

reaction time

readjusting

3. Save your work. You will use it again in the Vocabulary Check.

COLUMN 1	COLUMN 2
catnaps	how long it takes you to respond to something
functions	short periods of rest
internal "clock"	changing
reaction time	actions or purposes
readjusting	the part of the brain that controls different body activities

Strategy Builder

Outlining Main Ideas and Supporting Details

- You already know that most informational articles describe a particular **topic**, or subject. You also know that most informational articles are organized according to **main ideas** and **supporting details**. These ideas and details help explain or support the topic.

- There are many ways to keep track of main ideas and details as you read. In Lesson 3 you learned to summarize them. In Lesson 9 you learned to use an outline. An outline can be helpful when you do research, plan your own writing, or study for a test. Some outlines use a system or Roman numerals (I, II, III, IV, V, and so on) and capital letters (A, B, C, D, E, and so on).

- Read the following paragraphs, which tell why salt is important. Then read the outline of the paragraphs. Note how the main ideas are identified with Roman numerals, and the supporting details are shown with capital letters.

Salt

Salt is important for many reasons: It is a mineral that we need in order to say healthy. For thousands of years, we've used salt to season food. And before refrigerators were invented, salt was used to preserve food.

In the first century A.D., Roman soldiers were paid in salt. Our word *salary* comes from *sal,* which means "salt" in Latin.

I. Salt is important for many reasons.
  A. It's a mineral needed for staying healthy.
  B. It is used for seasoning food.
  C. It was used for preserving food.
  D. It was used to pay Roman soldiers.

Feeling Sleepy?

As you read this article, notice how it is organized. Think about how you might show the main ideas and supporting details in an outline.

"I have to be dragged out of bed," says Paul, 9. "It would take 20 alarm clocks to get me up."

Paul is not alone. Mara, 8, says her dad drags her out of bed, too. In fact, when we talked to kids, we discovered that the one thing you hate more than going to bed is getting up in the morning.

The reason: You need more sleep! The kids we surveyed get anywhere from 45 to 75 minutes too little sleep each night.

Zombie Zone

Missing Z's can create big problems. "When I'm sleepy, I can't do much," says Rosalie, 9. "I walk with my eyelids drooping."

Scientists aren't exactly sure why sleep is so important. Many think sleep helps our muscles repair themselves and gives our brains time to store "data" received during the day. Sleep may also help us fight disease. (That could explain why having a cold makes you feel like snoozing all day.)

One thing is certain. "Not getting enough sleep affects every part of your life," says Dr. Mary Carskadon, a scientist who studies snoozers. Sleepy kids have difficulty concentrating on school, friends—even on baseballs zooming past their noses.

Drooping Grades

"Sometimes during school, I put my head on my desk and drift off," says Elizabeth, 11. Desktop **catnaps** might make you feel better. But they might also show up on your report card. According to Dr. Carskadon's research, kids who earn mainly A's and B's go to bed earlier than those who get D's and F's. In one study, kids who got bad grades slept about 35 minutes less each night than their honor-roll classmates.

Friendship Fumbles

Losing sleep may also mean losing friends. Why? Because sleep may help kids control their emotions, says sleep researcher Carol Leotta. Lack of slumber can lead to more fights with friends, family, teachers, and others.

 Stop here for the Strategy Break.

Strategy Break

If you were to outline the main ideas and supporting details in this article so far, your outline might look something like this:

Feeling Sleepy?

I. Missing Z's (sleep) can create big problems—when you're sleepy, you can't do much.
II. Scientists aren't sure why sleep is so important.
   A. It may help our muscles repair.
   B. It may give our brains time to store "data" received during the day.
   C. It may help us fight disease.
III. Not getting enough sleep affects every part of kids' lives.
   A. They may have trouble concentrating on school.
   B. They may have trouble concentrating on friends.
   C. They may have trouble concentrating on sports.
IV. Desktop catnaps might make you feel better, but they might show up on your report card.
   A. According to research, kids who get mainly A's and B's go to bed earlier than kids who get D's and F's.
   B. In one study, kids who got bad grades slept 35 minutes less than kids on the honor roll.
V. Losing sleep may also mean losing friends.

 Go on reading.

Sports Strikeout

If you want to be a high scorer on your basketball team, you can forget catching the "Late Show." Dr. Carskadon says, "Not getting enough sleep slows your *reaction time*." That's how long it takes you to respond to something in your environment, like an opening on the court or a clear shot for the basket. To speed up your reactions and improve your game, take a tip from the pros: Go to bed early the night before the game.

Double Whammy

But the kids we talked to say it's not that easy: After-school sports practices, TV, and loads of homework make it tough to get to bed on time. "And when I spend the night at a friend's, we usually stay up until about 2 A.M.," added Pat.

These "social" reasons for staying awake are only half the problem, says Dr. Carskadon. Her research shows that as your body matures, your brain waits until later at night to release a chemical that makes you sleepy. In other words, it's natural for teens and almost-teens to crawl into bed and fall asleep later.

Pulling the Plug

Staying up later would be no big deal if you could wake up later, too. You'd just be resetting your **internal "clock"** (the part of your brain that controls your body's **functions**) to run on a later schedule. But if you drag yourself out of bed for an early-morning soccer game or to catch the school bus, you can expect to feel like a zombie.

That's because all sleep is not equal. The last hour of sleep, like the highest level on a video game, is worth more. But getting to that high level requires sleeping through all the lower levels first. Waking up too soon is like pulling the plug in the middle of the game.

Sleep Solutions

One way to make sure you get enough sleep is to stick to a regular schedule. It will be easier to fall asleep—and get up—if you go to bed at the same time every night.

Elizabeth tried to end her school-day snoozes by going to bed earlier—at 8:30 instead of 9:45. The change wasn't an immediate success, however. "Last night, I was in bed by 8:30," she reported. "But I finally got to sleep at about 11 o'clock."

If you want to reset your bedtime, Dr. Carskadon says, you need to be patient. Your internal clock is easy to set to a later sleep time—but **readjusting** to an earlier schedule is more challenging. For the best results, try moving your bedtime 15 minutes earlier each night.

Soothing music may also help. Max, 12, puts on a CD and says, "I'm usually asleep halfway through." Scientists also say to avoid exercise right before bed. And stay away from sugary foods; the energy boost might make you think you're not tired.

Afternoon naps can also help you feel well rested. Just make sure you don't nap too close to bedtime. That can make falling asleep at night harder.

The good news: You won't always need as much sleep as you do now. Most adults would be happy with an eight-hour snooze. So enjoy your Z's while you can! ●

Strategy Follow-up

Work with a group of classmates and create an outline for the second part of this article. Be sure to include only the most important ideas, and skip unnecessary details. If you can, compare your outline with those of other groups. See if your outlines all contain similar information. Change your group's outline if necessary.

✓Personal Checklist

Read each question and put a check (✓) in the correct box.

1. How well were you able to use the chart in Building Background to decide if you get enough sleep?
   ☐ 3 (extremely well)
   ☐ 2 (fairly well)
   ☐ 1 (not well)

2. By the time you finished reading this article, how well were you able to match the vocabulary words and their definitions?
   ☐ 3 (extremely well)
   ☐ 2 (fairly well)
   ☐ 1 (not well)

3. How well do you understand how sleep helps your body?
   ☐ 3 (extremely well)
   ☐ 2 (fairly well)
   ☐ 1 (not well)

4. How well do you understand the effects of not getting enough sleep?
   ☐ 3 (extremely well)
   ☐ 2 (fairly well)
   ☐ 1 (not well)

5. In the Strategy Follow-up, how well were you able to help your group outline the second part of the article?
   ☐ 3 (extremely well)
   ☐ 2 (fairly well)
   ☐ 1 (not well)

Vocabulary Check

Look back at the work you did in the Vocabulary Builder. Then answer each question by circling the correct letter.

1. What does your internal "clock" do?
   a. controls your body's functions
   b. lets you know how old you're getting
   c. lets you know what time it is

2. Which phrase best defines a catnap?
   a. a body function
   b. a short period of rest
   c. the time it takes to respond to something

3. Which word best describes what you are doing when you move your bedtime 15 minutes earlier each night?
   a. functioning
   b. readjusting
   c. catnapping

4. Which of these body functions are affected by sleep?
   a. concentration and memory
   b. coordination and muscle tone
   c. all of the above

5. What is an example of good reaction time?
   a. not hitting a ball that has been pitched to you
   b. catching a glass of milk before it spills
   c. both of the above

Add the numbers that you just checked to get your Personal Checklist score. Fill in your score here. Then turn to page 205 and transfer your score onto Graph 1.

Personal		
Vocabulary		
Strategy		
Comprehension		
TOTAL SCORE		

✓ T

Check your answers with your teacher. Give yourself 1 point for each correct answer, and fill in your Vocabulary score here. Then turn to page 205 and transfer your score onto Graph 1.

Personal		
Vocabulary		
Strategy		
Comprehension		
TOTAL SCORE		

✓ T

Strategy Check

Review the outline that your group completed during the Strategy Follow-up. Then answer these questions:

1. Which detail describes how to speed up your reaction time when you play sports?
   a. Go to bed early the night before a game.
   b. Move your bedtime 15 minutes earlier each night.
   c. Make sure you don't nap too close to bedtime.

2. Which section of the article includes details about resetting your bedtime?
   a. "Sports Strikeout"
   b. "Double Whammy"
   c. "Sleep Solutions"

3. Which main idea can be found in the section called "Double Whammy"?
   a. There are many reasons why kids don't get to bed on time.
   b. If you want to be a high scorer, you've got to get enough sleep.
   c. Staying up late would be no big deal if you could wake up later, too.

4. Which section of the articles includes details about the importance of the last hour of sleep?
   a. "Double Whammy"
   b. "Pulling the Plug"
   c. "Sleep Solutions"

5. What would *not* be a main idea in the section called "Sleep Solutions"?
   a. One way to get enough sleep is to stick to a regular schedule.
   b. If you want to reset your bedtime, you need to be patient.
   c. Waking up too soon is like pulling the plug in the middle of a video game.

Comprehension Check

Review the article if necessary. Then answer these questions:

1. In what way does sleep affect relationships?
   a. It improves reaction times.
   b. It helps control emotions.
   c. It resets your internal clock.

2. Why is it hard for teens and almost-teens to fall asleep early?
   a. Their brain waits until later at night to release a chemical that makes them sleepy.
   b. Their brain releases a chemical that makes them want to stay awake all night.
   c. Their brain waits until early in the morning to release a chemical that makes them sleepy.

3. How would you reset your internal clock so you could get to sleep earlier?
   a. Stay up until 2:00 A.M. one night, and go to bed at 9:00 P.M. the next night.
   b. Go to bed 15 minutes earlier each night until you reach your desired bedtime.
   c. Keep your bedtime routine exactly the same every night.

4. Which of the following statements is true?
   a. Your last hour of sleep doesn't provide any benefits.
   b. Your last hour of sleep provides the least benefits.
   c. Your last hour of sleep provides the most benefits.

5. After reading this article, what might you do before bed to help you fall asleep?
   a. Eat some chocolate chip cookies.
   b. Listen to some soothing music.
   c. Play a fast game of basketball.

Check your answers with your teacher. Give yourself 1 point for each correct answer, and fill in your Strategy score here. Then turn to page 205 and transfer your score onto Graph 1.

Check your answers with your teacher. Give yourself 1 point for each correct answer, and fill in your Comprehension score here. Then turn to page 205 and transfer your score onto Graph 1.

Extending

Choose one or both of these activities:

CHART YOUR SLEEP FOR A WEEK

Make a chart to track how much sleep you get in one week. For seven days in a row, record what time you went to sleep and what time you woke up. At the end of the seven days, determine the amount of sleep you got each night, and then average the number of hours. Use the chart in Building Background to help you decide if you are getting the amount of sleep that you need for your age.

RESET YOUR INTERNAL CLOCK

If you aren't getting enough sleep, consider using the suggestions in "Feeling Sleepy?" to reset your own internal clock. Plan the changes that you want to make and how you want to make them. Some of the resources listed on this page might help you get started. As you go through the process of readjusting your schedule, record any noticeable effects in a "sleep log" that you keep by your bed.

Resources

Books

Who Needs to Sleep Anyway! How Animals Sleep by Colin Shapiro. Copyright © 1996 by Black Moss Press.

Sleep on It! by Kevin Kelly and Erin Jaeb. Copyright © 1995 by Children's Press.

Music

Maiden of Mysteries: The Music of Enya performed by Taliesin Orchestra and Enya. Copyright © 1998 by Platinum Distribution.

Beethoven: The String Quartets/Emerson String Quartet performed by Emerson String Quartet. Copyright © 1997 by Pgd/Deutsche Grammophon—# 447075.

Mozart for Morning Meditation—Serene Serenade for the Soul performed by Academy of St. Martin in the Fields members, Hagen String Quartet, Sabine Meyer, Mitsuko Uchida, et al. Copyright © 1998 by Pgd/Philips—# 462710.

The Mozart Effect: Music for Children, Vols. 1–3 [Box Set] performed by various artists. Copyright © 1997 by WEA Atlantic Children's Group—#84259.

White Stones by Secret Garden. Copyright © 1997 by Pgd/Polygram Pop/Jazz.

How to Be a Super Sorter: Five Steps for Managing the Mess

Building Background

"Clean your room!" How many times have you heard *that* before? Work with a small group to brainstorm and share ideas for how to clean your room. Have one person record your ideas on a large concept map, or web. When you finish reading "How to Be a Super Sorter," return to your web and compare your ideas with those presented in the article.

keepsakes

monumental

tackle

tidy

train

whirlwind

Vocabulary Builder

1. Before you read "How to Be a Super Sorter," read the vocabulary words in the margin. If you do not know what any of the words mean, look them up in a dictionary.

2. Then underline the word or phrase in each row that is a synonym of the boldfaced vocabulary word. (Reminder: A **synonym** is a word that has the same meaning as another word.)

keepsakes	bits of trash	souvenirs
monumental	huge	small
tackle	show off	take on
tidy	sloppy	neat
train	teach	forget
whirlwind	flood	tornado

3. Save your work. You will use it again in the Vocabulary Check.

Strategy Builder

Following the Steps in a Process

- A **"how-to" article** is an article that tells readers how to do or make something. An author's purpose for writing a how-to article is always to **inform**. How-to articles include steps for doing or making things. These steps are written in a particular order, or **sequence**. It is important to follow the steps in their exact order. Otherwise you could end up doing things incorrectly.

- Read the following paragraphs, which explain how to arrange your CDs. Pay attention to the sequence of the steps.

Can you find your favorite compact disc? It's probably in your CD player! But what about all of your other CDs? Follow these steps to organize your CDs, and you'll be moving to the music like never before!

1. **Put CDs in their jewel cases.** Begin by finding all of the jewel cases. Then put each CD in its correct case. Broken or missing jewel cases? You can buy extras at a computer or music store.

2. **Decide where to keep your CDs.** Use the space you have to decide how will you organize and display your CDs. Try to find a box or shelf that will hold them all in one place. Most music stores have inexpensive CD holders.

3. **Put your CDs in order.** Alphabetize your CDs by title or artist. Or organize them by type of music.

Now you can enjoy *all* of your music because you will be able to find whatever you're in the mood to listen to!

- You can show the steps in this process on a **sequence chain**. It would look like this:

1 Put CDs in their jewel cases.
- Put each CD in its correct jewel case.
- If cases are broken or missing, buy extras at a computer or music store.

2 Decide where to keep your CDs.
- Decide how you will organize and display your CDs.
- Try to find a box or shelf that will hold them all in one place.

3 Put your CDs in order.
- Alphabetize your CDs by title or artist.
- Or organize them by type of music.

How to Be a Super Sorter: Five Steps for Managing the Mess

By Edith H. Fine and Judith P. Josephson

As you read the beginning of this article, apply the strategies that you just learned. Think about how you could show the steps in this process on a sequence chain.

So your room is a pile of unfinished projects, unsorted papers, a soccer jersey from last fall, and—beneath it all—puzzle pieces and hamster food. You catch a whiff of old banana peel and dirty socks every time you walk in the door, and you can't see the top of your bed. "No baseball until your room is clean!" your parents say.

Some kids seem to be born tidy. But if you were not, you probably hear "clean your room" and think "cram piles under the bed and into the closet." You also know, though, that this kind of cleaning is just a quick fix.

Wouldn't you like to clean up your room for good? A *real* clean-up job is not such a monumental task if you learn a few timesaving "tricks of the trade."

If you share a room, get your brother or sister to help. Then collect a pile of big boxes, haul them and a kitchen timer into your room, and you're ready for the five easy steps that will turn *you* into a super sorter!

1 Do a "Big Sort."

Think about what's in that tangle of stuff in your room:

- clothes
- toys and games
- school supplies
- big stuff
- books and magazines
- sports equipment
- important papers
- not-so-important papers
- candy wrappers that never quite got thrown away

A big job seems smaller when it's broken into chunks. Label the empty boxes with the above big group names (or whatever categories fit the contents of your room). Write "Give Away" on one box for things you don't want. Draw a big "?" on another box for those things that don't belong anywhere else.

Set the timer for 60 minutes. Working for just an hour at a time, you won't feel as if you're climbing a mountain of messiness. Ready, set, *GO*! Put letters from friends and unsorted school papers into a "Papers" box. Stash shin guards in with "Sports Equipment." Throw stinky socks and dirty sweatshirts in a laundry basket. Hang up clothes that belong in the closet. Keep going! Pair your shoes and line them up next to your bed (or in your closet, if there's room). Put dirty dishes in the hall to take to the kitchen later. Take a look around. There's your bed! Dad's missing hammer! Tuesday's homework assignment! Things are getting neater. Toss trash into the wastebasket.

Depending on how messy your room is, this Big Sort could take several sessions. Keep at it!

2 Plan where things should live.

Tackle one of your Big Sort groups at a time. Do the items in your groups already have a home, and they just aren't in it? Or do they need "a place to call home"?

Dirty clothes, for example: If you usually toss them on the floor, put a clothes basket behind your door. Ready, aim . . . shoot your clothes into the basket. Score!

Store similar supplies in one place. Desk supplies can go into the bottom and lid of an empty egg carton. Put puzzle pieces in small empty gift boxes. Stash hobby supplies in labeled plastic bags or tubs.

Draw a map of your room to figure out where to put things. Once everything has a home, you can train yourself to put items in their place as soon as you're done with them. That makes it much easier to keep your room neat.

 Stop here for the Strategy Break.

Strategy Break

If you wanted to begin a sequence chain to show the steps in the process of cleaning your room, it might look like this:

1 **Do a "Big Sort."**

- Label boxes with categories that fit the contents of your room.
- Set the timer for 60 minutes.
- Sort things into the boxes, and put things away as you go.
- Take as many sessions as you need to do the Big Sort.

2 **Plan where things should live.**

- Tackle one Big Sort group at a time, and give the items in each group a home.
- Draw a map of your room to figure out where to put things.
- Train yourself to put things in their homes as soon as you are done with them.

To be continued . . .

 Go on reading.

3 Decide what to keep or toss.

Do you really want the poster you bought two summers ago? The ticket stub from last week's movie? The sweatshirt you wore in kindergarten? Start a box for "Keepsakes"—things you'd like to keep but never use.

For "I don't know" papers, put a future date (perhaps six months from now) in the corner and put them to one side on your desk. If you haven't looked at the papers by that date, toss them.

4 Make cleaning a habit.

Every day for at least three weeks, practice putting things in their "homes" after you've used them. As soon as you come in from school, for example, drop off your lunch box in the kitchen, hang your jacket on a hook, and put your homework on your desk. After you've done your homework, put away books and pencils, and sort papers into neat stacks.

In addition to daily cleaning, work like a whirlwind on your Big Sort boxes for 30 minutes each Saturday until you have gone through the contents of each one.

5 **Take it one step at a time.**

Don't be discouraged if your room gets messy again. It takes time to develop a new habit.

But once things are in place, you'll be able to vacuum and dust much faster. Things will be easier to find. Mom and Dad will be very impressed. And visitors won't catch a whiff of banana-and-gym-sock perfume as they approach your room. ●

Strategy Follow-up

First, look back that the concept map that your group created in Building Background. How do your ideas for cleaning your room compare with the ones in the article?

Next, work with a partner to finish the sequence chain for this article. Begin by copying Steps 1 and 2 onto a large sheet of paper. Add boxes for Steps 3–5, and then take turns filling in the information.

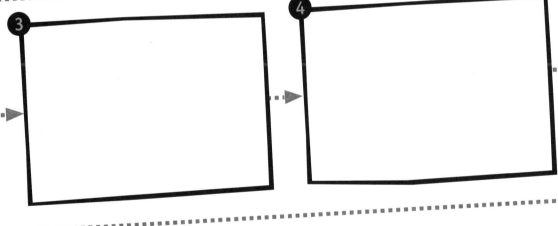

1

Do a "Big Sort."

- Label boxes with categories that fit the contents of your room.
- Set the timer for 60 minutes.
- Sort things into the boxes, and put things away as you go.
- Take as many sessions as you need to do the Big Sort.

2

Plan where things should live.

- Tackle one Big Sort group at a time, and give the items in each group a home.
- Draw a map of your room to figure out where to put things.
- Train yourself to put things in their homes as soon as you are done with them.

3

4

5

✓Personal Checklist

Read each question and put a check (✓) in the correct box.

1. In Building Background, how well were you able to come up with ideas for how to clean your room?
   - ☐ 3 (extremely well)
   - ☐ 2 (fairly well)
   - ☐ 1 (not well)

2. In the Vocabulary Builder, how well were you able to find the synonym of each vocabulary word?
   - ☐ 3 (extremely well)
   - ☐ 2 (fairly well)
   - ☐ 1 (not well)

3. Now that you've read this article, how well could you follow the steps in it to clean your own room?
   - ☐ 3 (extremely well)
   - ☐ 2 (fairly well)
   - ☐ 1 (not well)

4. How well do you understand the importance of "finding a home" for all of your things?
   - ☐ 3 (extremely well)
   - ☐ 2 (fairly well)
   - ☐ 1 (not well)

5. How well were you able to complete the sequence chain in the Strategy Follow-up?
   - ☐ 3 (extremely well)
   - ☐ 2 (fairly well)
   - ☐ 1 (not well)

Vocabulary Check

Look back at the work you did in the Vocabulary Builder. Then answer each question by circling the correct letter.

1. What is a synonym for the word *tidy*?
   - a. dirty
   - b. neat
   - c. sloppy

2. Which of these things would you describe as monumental?
   - a. a tiny ant
   - b. a huge mountain
   - c. a minivan

3. Which of these might you put into a box of keepsakes?
   - a. pictures
   - b. trash
   - c. paper clips

4. When might a person act like a whirlwind?
   - a. when he or she is falling asleep
   - b. when he or she is in a big hurry
   - c. when he or she is taking a bath

5. What is another way of saying, "tackle a job"?
   - a. take on a task
   - b. take a break
   - c. knock down a box

Add the numbers that you just checked to get your Personal Checklist score. Fill in your score here. Then turn to page 205 and transfer your score onto Graph 1.

Personal		
Vocabulary		
Strategy		
Comprehension		
TOTAL SCORE		
	✓	T

Check your answers with your teacher. Give yourself 1 point for each correct answer, and fill in your Vocabulary score here. Then turn to page 205 and transfer your score onto Graph 1.

Personal		
Vocabulary		
Strategy		
Comprehension		
TOTAL SCORE		
	✓	T

Strategy Check

Review the sequence chain that you completed in the Strategy Follow-up. Then answer these questions:

1. What is one of the things that Step 3 suggests for deciding what to keep or toss?
   a. Practice putting things into their homes.
   b. Start a box for "Keepsakes" that you never use.
   c. Don't be discouraged if your room gets messy again.

2. In which step would you find the suggestion to make a box for "I don't know" papers?
   a. Step 3
   b. Step 4
   c. Step 5

3. Which step suggests working on your Big Sort boxes for 30 minutes every Saturday?
   a. Step 3
   b. Step 4
   c. Step 5

4. What does Step 5 suggest?
   a. Decide what to keep or toss.
   b. Make cleaning a habit.
   c. Take it one step at a time.

5. Why is it important to follow the steps in this article in the exact order that they are given?
   a. The process won't work if the steps are out of order.
   b. It's not important—you can follow the steps in any order.
   c. It will take you much longer if you do the steps out of order.

Comprehension Check

Review the article if necessary. Then answer these questions:

1. Why do the authors suggest setting a timer while you clean your room?
   a. Working for an hour at a time makes a big job seem smaller.
   b. An hour is all the time it will take to clean your entire room.
   c. Whatever you haven't cleaned in an hour isn't worth keeping.

2. What do the authors say will help you "find homes" for all of your things?
   a. vacuuming your rug
   b. drawing a map of your room
   c. throwing away boxes

3. How often do the authors say you should clean in order to get into the habit?
   a. every day for at least one week
   b. every day for at least two weeks
   c. every day for at least three weeks

4. What do the authors say you should you do every Saturday?
   a. clean your entire room
   b. find new homes for things
   c. empty the Big Sort boxes

5. Why shouldn't you get discouraged if your room gets messy again?
   a. Cleaning it is a waste of time anyway.
   b. It takes time to develop a new habit.
   c. It will never stay clean, so why bother?

Check your answers with your teacher. Give yourself 1 point for each correct answer, and fill in your Strategy score here. Then turn to page 205 and transfer your score onto Graph 1.

Personal		
Vocabulary		
Strategy		
Comprehension		
TOTAL SCORE		

✓ T

Check your answers with your teacher. Give yourself 1 point for each correct answer, and fill in your Comprehension score here. Then turn to page 205 and transfer your score onto Graph 1.

Personal		
Vocabulary		
Strategy		
Comprehension		
TOTAL SCORE		

✓ T

Extending

Choose one or more of these activities:

WRITE A HOW-TO ARTICLE

Think of something that you know how to do well. Create a sequence chain that shows all of the steps in the process. Then use your sequence chain to write a how-to article. Read your article aloud, and if possible, demonstrate the process for the class.

LEARN A NEW SKILL

Use one of the how-to books listed on this page, and follow the steps to make or do something new.

WATCH A HOW-TO VIDEO

Use the how-to video listed on this page, or videotape someone making or doing something on a TV show. Write down the steps involved in the process. You might need to pause, rewind, or watch the tape several times to make sure you get all the steps. Then put the steps on a sequence chain, and let someone else read it. Can that person follow the sequence clearly? Why or why not?

USE THIS ARTICLE TO CLEAN AND SORT YOUR ROOM

Take a "before" picture of your room, or draw one. Then use the sequence chain that you created for this article to sort and clean your room. Keep a log of what you did for each step. Then take or draw an "after" picture. Include the pictures in your log, as well as any additional tips that you come up with for sorting and cleaning. Share your log with a classmate or classmates.

Resources

How-to Books

Bicycling: How to Play the All-Star Way by John Francis. Copyright © 1998 by Raintree/Steck-Vaughn.

Camy Baker's How to Be Popular in the Sixth Grade by Camy Baker. Copyright © 1998 by Bantam Books.

Chess for Kids: How to Play (And How to Win!) by Conn McQuinn. Copyright © 1998 by Troll Associates.

Funny You Should Ask: How to Make Up Jokes and Riddles with Wordplay by Marvin Terban and John O'Brien. Copyright © 1992 by Houghton Mifflin Co.

The American Boy's Handy Book: What to Do and How to Do It by Daniel C. Beard. Copyright © 1998 by David R. Godin.

Video

Kids Make Puppets—Easy Scarf Marionettes starring Jim Gamble Puppets. Copyright © 1997. ASIN: 1890544914.

Dracula (Part 1)

Building Background

A **play** is writing that is meant to be performed or read aloud. When you read a play, it helps to imagine that you are acting in a performance.

When you watch or read a play, the characters should seem very real. A **character** in a play is acted by a real person. That person uses his or her tone of voice, facial expressions, and movements to bring the character to life. If possible, read both parts of *Dracula* aloud with a group of classmates. (You will read Part 2 in the next lesson.) Think about how you would read the part so that you bring your character to life.

horror

property

foreboding

Count Dracula

fury

rosary

vanishes

vision

transforms

vampire

Vocabulary Builder

1. Read the words in the margin, and then use them to help you predict what might happen in *Dracula,* Part 1.

2. Write your prediction on a separate sheet of paper, and use as many vocabulary words as possible. If you don't know some of the words, look them up in a dictionary.

3. Save your work. You will use it again in the Vocabulary Check.

Strategy Builder

Identifying Mood

• A **play** has certain elements, or parts. Many of the elements in plays are similar to elements in fictional stories. For example, both plays and stories often have a **setting**, a **narrator** who tells the story, **characters** who perform the action, and a **plot** that includes a **problem** and **solutions**.

- Both plays and stories often create certain **moods** too. For example, mysteries have suspenseful moods, and comedies have silly moods. By paying attention to the mood, the audience can often predict what might happen in a play.

- Read the following paragraph, which describes the opening scene of a play. Note the descriptive details that help create the mood.

In the opening scene of the play, a very fat man is riding on a squeaky old bus. He is bouncing up and down, and his hat keeps falling over his eyes. Every time he tries to straighten his hat, he drops something out of his hands. When the people sitting around him try to hand him the things he has dropped, he drops something else. A little girl who is watching the man is giggling behind a book. Some of the adults are smiling too.

- If you wanted to list the details that describe the mood of this scene, you could put them on a **chart** like the one below. Using these details, would you predict that something funny or serious is going to happen in this play?

Details that Help Create the Mood	
Details that Describe the Bus	• squeaky • old
Details that Describe the Man	• very fat • bouncing up and down • hat keeps falling over his eyes • keeps dropping things
Details that Describe the Other People on the Bus	• little girl is giggling behind a book • some of the adults are smiling too

Dracula (Part 1)

a play based on Bram Stoker's classic novel, first published more than 100 years ago

This play has an unusual feature: the characters' diaries have roles of their own. Each diary tells what a character is thinking and helps create the mood of the play. As you read Part 1 of *Dracula*, note the details that describe the mood.

CHARACTERS:

Narrator 1

Narrator 2

Jonathan Harker, a young lawyer

Harker's Diary

Count Dracula

PART I: TRANSYLVANIA

Scene 1

Narrator 1: The following is a story of **horror** almost too terrible to imagine. But all of it is true. Even if you are a skeptic, and slow to believe your eyes, read this tale and beware. It tells of a world of undead restless souls who thrive on the blood of others. And, dear reader, it is the same world in which you walk each day!

Narrator 2: Our story begins in the year 1897. Jonathan Harker, a young English lawyer, is sent to the remote Eastern European country of Transylvania. There, he is to meet a mysterious **Count Dracula**, who is buying **property** in England. During his visit, Harker keeps a diary, which will help to tell our story.

Harker's Diary: I was transported to Castle Dracula by coach. It was very late at night, and I could hardly see my surroundings. When the other riders heard where I was headed, they became terrified, saying strange words in their language, like "wampyre." Were they trying to warn me?

Narrator 1: Harker arrives at the dark, **foreboding** castle. He is greeted by a stranger.

Harker's Diary: There stood a tall old man with a long moustache. He was dressed in black from head to foot. Beckoning me inside, he spoke with a rather odd accent.

Dracula: Welcome to my house! Enter freely. Go safely, and leave something of the happiness you bring.

Harker's Diary: He grabbed my hand and shook it with the strength of a vise. Worse still, his hand was icy cold, like a dead person's. I shivered.

Harker: Count Dracula?

Dracula: I am Dracula. Come in. The night air is chill, and you must need to eat and rest.

Harker's Diary: He led me through many dark corridors and winding stairs. Finally, he threw open the door to a dining room.

Dracula: Please be seated and dine. Excuse me that I do not join you, but I have dined already.

Harker's Diary: After dinner, I answered his many questions about Carfax, the estate he is buying outside London. As we sat by a crackling fire in his sitting room, I was suddenly aware of the terrible howling of a pack of wolves outside the castle walls. It was a lonely, terrifying sound. But when I glanced at the Count, he smiled at me.

Dracula: Listen to them—the children of the night. What music they make!

Harker's Diary: He must have seen the nervousness on my face.

Dracula: Ah, sir. You city dwellers cannot understand the feelings of the hunter. Come, you must be tired. Your bedroom is waiting. Sleep as long as you like. I will be away until evening.

 Stop here for the Strategy Break.

Strategy Break

If you were to create a chart of details that describe the mood in Scene 1, your chart might look like this:

Details that Help Create the Mood in Scene 1	
Details that Describe Transylvania and its People	• world of restless souls who thrive on the blood of others • remote Eastern European country • people are terrified of Dracula and call him a "wampyre"
Details that Describe the Castle and its Surroundings	• very late at night—Harker could hardly see his surroundings • dark and foreboding castle • dark corridors and winding stairs • terrible howling of wolves—lonely, terrifying sound
Details that Describe Count Dracula	• mysterious old man • dressed in black from head to foot • hand is icy cold, like a dead person's

As you read Scenes 2 and 3, notice the descriptive words that continue to create the mood. In the Strategy Follow-up, you will create a chart for these scenes.

 Go on reading to see what happens.

Scene 2

Narrator 2: The next day, Harker sleeps until late afternoon.

Harker's Diary: I found myself alone in the enormous castle. I wanted to dress, but I could not find a single mirror anywhere. Finally, I found a small mirror in my toilet kit and began to shave.

Narrator 1: Suddenly, Harker senses a presence behind him. The Count is peering over his shoulder.

Harker's Diary: For some reason I had not seen him in my little mirror. His presence startled me. I cut my chin with my razor. A few drops of blood trickled forth.

Narrator 2: Seeing the blood, the Count's eyes flash with a strange and terrible **fury**. He lunges, his hand grasping for Harker's throat.

Harker's Diary: I flinched, and his hand caught on the **rosary** that I wear around my neck. Somehow, that seemed to change his mood, and he withdrew his hand and its jagged nails.

Dracula: Take care how you cut yourself. It is more dangerous than you think in this country.

Narrator 1: Then, as quietly as he arrived, the Count **vanishes**.

Harker's Diary: What kind of a man is my host? Why does he never eat? Where does he go all day? Why are there no mirrors here, and why did I not see him in my small mirror?

Narrator 2: Harker decides to search the castle for answers.

Harker's Diary: All I found was a maze of doors, doors, doors everywhere. Every one was locked and bolted. This castle has become a prison, and I fear that I am its prisoner!

Scene 3

Narrator 1: Late that night Harker is in his room when a strange **vision** appears to him. It is a beautiful woman in a flowing gown.

Harker's Diary: I wasn't sure if I was awake or asleep and dreaming. She kept coming closer to me. When she was just inches away, she opened her mouth to show razor-sharp teeth. I was trapped as she closed in on my neck. I felt her breath on my throat.

Narrator 2: Suddenly, a wolf appears, and **transforms** itself into Count Dracula. There are traces of blood around his mouth. His eyes are filled with fury and hate. He screams at the woman in an eerie, raspy voice.

Dracula: How dare you touch him after I have forbidden it! This man belongs to me. I told you, you are welcome to him in a month, when I am through with him. If I catch you in here again, you will pay dearly. Now away!

Narrator 1: He turns to Harker, who is still quite shaken.

Dracula: Try to forget that little unpleasantness, my friend. And do not worry. I need you alive and well to sell me that property. After that, of course, who knows?

Harker's Diary: Now it is all clear to me. Dracula is a **vampire**, an undead creature of the night, who drinks the blood of living humans to survive. He is determined to buy Carfax estate in England. For what reason, I do not know. It will take about a month for the sale to go through, and require my signature and expertise. After that, if I have not managed to escape, Dracula and that woman will surely drain my blood, and with it, my life. Oh, was ever a man in more desperate straits than I? •

Strategy Follow-up

On the chart below, list details from Scenes 2 and 3 that add to the mood of this play.

Details that Help Create the Mood in Scenes 2 and 3	
Details that Describe the Castle	
Details that Describe Count Dracula	
Details that Describe the Woman	

✓Personal Checklist

Read each question and put a check (✓) in the correct box.

1. How well do you understand the differences between a play and a fictional story?
   - ☐ 3 (extremely well)
   - ☐ 2 (fairly well)
   - ☐ 1 (not well)

2. In the Vocabulary Builder, how many vocabulary words were you able to use in your prediction?
   - ☐ 3 (7–10 words)
   - ☐ 2 (4–6 words)
   - ☐ 1 (0–3 words)

3. How well were you able to find words and phrases that describe the mood in Scenes 2 and 3?
   - ☐ 3 (extremely well)
   - ☐ 2 (fairly well)
   - ☐ 1 (not well)

4. How well do you understand why Jonathan Harker goes to Transylvania?
   - ☐ 3 (extremely well)
   - ☐ 2 (fairly well)
   - ☐ 1 (not well)

5. How well do you understand why Harker feels that he is in danger?
   - ☐ 3 (extremely well)
   - ☐ 2 (fairly well)
   - ☐ 1 (not well)

Vocabulary Check

Look back at the work you did in the Vocabulary Builder. Then answer each question by circling the correct letter.

1. Which vocabulary word could you have used to predict a feeling or mood of dread?
   - a. foreboding
   - b. transforms
   - c. vanishes

2. Which vocabulary words could you have used to best predict what Count Dracula would do?
   - a. property, horror
   - b. transforms, vampire
   - c. vision, rosary

3. Which word could you have used to predict how a character might feel?
   - a. vanishes
   - b. vampire
   - c. fury

4. What kind of event might the word *horror* predict?
   - a. something wonderful happening
   - b. something hilarious happening
   - c. something terrible happening

5. What does the word *transforms* mean?
   - a. something changes
   - b. something appears
   - c. something stops

Add the numbers that you just checked to get your Personal Checklist score. Fill in your score here. Then turn to page 205 and transfer your score onto Graph 1.

Personal	
Vocabulary	
Strategy	
Comprehension	
TOTAL SCORE	
	✓ T

Check your answers with your teacher. Give yourself 1 point for each correct answer, and fill in your Vocabulary score here. Then turn to page 205 and transfer your score onto Graph 1.

Personal	
Vocabulary	
Strategy	
Comprehension	
TOTAL SCORE	
	✓ T

Strategy Check

Review the chart that you created in the Strategy Follow-up. Then answer these questions:

1. Which of these words from the play best help describe the mood?

   a. true, dear, young

   b. mysterious, foreboding, terrible

   c. welcome, safely, happiness

2. Which quote from the play best helps describe the mood?

   a. "Try to forget that little unpleasantness, my friend."

   b. "Welcome to my house! Enter freely."

   c. "It is more dangerous than you think in this country."

3. Which of these phrases best shows the mood in Scene 3?

   a. little unpleasantness

   b. fury and hate

   c. both of the above

4. How does the mention of blood affect the mood of the play?

   a. Blood usually suggests injury or death.

   b. Blood usually refers to good health.

   c. Blood usually means the suspense is almost over.

5. Which phrase best suggests the overall mood at the end of *Dracula*, Part 1?

   a. desperate straits

   b. strange vision

   c. maze of doors

Comprehension Check

Review the selection if necessary. Then answer these questions:

1. Why is Jonathan Harker in Transylvania?

   a. He is trying to get Dracula to help him become a vampire.

   b. He is looking for property to buy in Transylvania.

   c. He is trying to help Dracula buy property in England.

2. Which quote or sentence best reveals Dracula's true personality?

   a. "Enter freely. Go safely, and leave something of the happiness you bring."

   b. Seeing the blood, the Count's eyes flash with a strange and terrible fury.

   c. "You must be tired. Your bedroom is waiting. Sleep as long as you like."

3. Why does Dracula lunge at Harker?

   a. He wants to steal Harker's razor.

   b. He sees blood on Harker's chin.

   c. He tries to keep Harker from cutting himself.

4. When does Harker become sure that Dracula is a vampire?

   a. right after Dracula lunges at him

   b. when a woman attacks him

   c. after he sees a wolf transform into Dracula

5. Why does Dracula tell the woman she is welcome to Harker in a month?

   a. Dracula needs Harker's help for about a month to buy property in England.

   b. Harker won't have any blood left after a month, so Dracula won't need him.

   c. He's trying to trick the woman. Harker will be back in England before then.

Check your answers with your teacher. Give yourself 1 point for each correct answer, and fill in your Strategy score here. Then turn to page 205 and transfer your score onto Graph 1.

Personal	
Vocabulary	
Strategy	
Comprehension	
TOTAL SCORE	✓ T

Check your answers with your teacher. Give yourself 1 point for each correct answer, and fill in your Comprehension score here. Then turn to page 205 and transfer your score onto Graph 1.

Personal	
Vocabulary	
Strategy	
Comprehension	
TOTAL SCORE	✓ T

Extending

Choose one or both of these activities:

CREATE THE SET OF DRACULA

Create a sketch or model of the set that you would use to stage a performance of *Dracula*. Use descriptions from the play and your own imagination to create your set.

CHOOSE BACKGROUND MUSIC FOR THE PLAY

When a play contains background music, the mood is often stronger. Listen to some recordings, and find music that would help convey the mood of *Dracula*. (Some of the recordings listed on this page might give you a place to start.) Or if you'd like, you can play the music yourself and record it. Then, as you and your classmates read Part 1 aloud, play the music that you have chosen or recorded. How does it help to make the mood stronger?

Resources

Books

A Terrifying Taste of Short and Shivery: Thirty Creepy Tales by Robert San Souci. Copyright © 1998 by Delacorte Press.

Even More Short and Shivery by Robert San Souci. Copyright © 1999 by Bantam Books.

Hook Moon Night: Spooky Tales from the Georgia Mountains by Faye Gibbons. Copyright © 1997 by William Morrow and Company.

Tales to Give You Goosebumps: Ten Spooky Stories by R. L. Stine. Copyright © 1997 by Scholastic Paperbacks.

Music

Highlights from the Phantom of the Opera: The Original Cast Recording by Andrew Lloyd Webber. Copyright © 1988 Pgd/Polygram Pop/Jazz.

Star Wars Episode I: The Phantom Menace by John Williams. Copyright © 1999 by Sony Music.

Vertigo: Original Motion Picture Score by Bernard Herrmann. Copyright © 1996 by Uni/Varese Sarahande.

LESSON 15

Dracula (Part 2)

Building Background

From *Dracula*, Part 1:

Narrator 2: *Suddenly, a wolf appears, and transforms itself into Count Dracula. There are traces of blood around his mouth. His eyes are filled with fury and hate. He screams at the woman in an eerie, raspy voice.*

Dracula: *How dare you touch him after I have forbidden it! This man belongs to me. I told you, you are welcome to him in a month, when I am through with him. If I catch you in here again, you will pay dearly. Now away!*

Narrator 1: *He turns to Harker, who is still quite shaken.*

Dracula: *Try to forget that little unpleasantness, my friend. And do not worry. I need you alive and well to sell me that property. After that, of course, who knows?*

Harker's Diary: *Now it is all clear to me. Dracula is a vampire, an undead creature of the night, who drinks the blood of living humans to survive. He is determined to buy Carfax estate in England. For what reason, I do not know. It will take about a month for the sale to go through, and require my signature and expertise. After that, if I have not managed to escape, Dracula and that woman will surely drain my blood, and with it, my life. Oh, was ever a man in more desperate straits than I?*

crucifix

eternity

haunted

hypnotize

intrusion

witnesses

stake

Vocabulary Builder

1. The boldfaced vocabulary words below are from Part 2 of *Dracula*. Read each boldfaced word, and then underline the best synonym for it. (Reminder: **Synonyms** have nearly the same meaning.)

crucifix	nail	cross	rosary
eternity	forever	never	ending
haunted	closed	dusty	spooky
hypnotize	lie to	put in a trance	bore to tears

intrusion	invasion	separation	reunion
witnesses	observers	women	sleepwalkers
stake	meat	mail	stick

2. Save your work. You will use it again in the Vocabulary Check.

Strategy Builder

Using Foreshadowing to Predict

- As you know, *Dracula* is a mystery. **Mysteries** always contain some kind of puzzle or problem that the characters must solve. Mysteries also contain suspense. Authors create **suspense** by not giving too much away. They leave it up to their audience to figure things out and solve the mystery.

- One of the ways authors create suspense is by using foreshadowing. **Foreshadowing** is when an author provides clues about something before it happens. If readers are really paying attention, they can use these clues to **predict** what will happen. This helps them solve the mystery.

- Note the foreshadowing in this passage from Part 1 of *Dracula:*

> **Harker's Diary:** I was transported to Castle Dracula by coach. It was very late at night, and I could hardly see my surroundings. When the other riders heard where I was headed, they became terrified, saying strange words in their language, like "wampyre." Were they trying to warn me?
>
> **Narrator 1**: Harker arrives at the dark, foreboding castle. He is greeted by a stranger.

- In Building Background you reread the end of *Dracula,* Part 1. How does the passage above foreshadow Harker's discovery that Dracula is a vampire?

_____

_____

_____

_____

Dracula (Part 2)

a play based on Bram Stoker's classic novel, first published more than 100 years ago

Read on to find out how things will turn out in this mystery play. Pay careful attention to the foreshadowing that the author provides. It will help you make predictions while you read.

CHARACTERS:

Narrator 1

Narrator 2

Jonathan Harker, a young lawyer

Harker's Diary

Count Dracula

Mina Murray, Jonathan Harker's fiancée

Mina's Journal

Dr. John Seward

Seward's Journal

Mr. Renfield, a mental patient

Professor Van Helsing, a doctor from Amsterdam

Van Helsing's Journal

Maid

Attendant

Newspaper Article

PART II: ENGLAND

Scene 4

Narrator 2: At this very same time, Harker's fiancée, Mina Murray, has just arrived in the town of Whitby, on the English seashore.

Mina's Journal: I'm ever so glad to be back. Just think, a whole summer here in paradise. One sad note: still no word from my poor Jonathan. His firm received a note from Count Dracula saying that he requires Jonathan's help for another month. But I can't help worrying about him. It's not like Jonathan to be out of touch for so long. I guess I won't become Mrs. Jonathan Harker until the fall.

Narrator 1: The next day, Mina visits her friend Dr. Seward at his house on the grounds of a mental hospital that he runs.

Seward: It's lovely to see you again, Mina. Remember when you were little, you used to think that Carfax, the estate next door, was **haunted**?

Mina: Oh, John, I was just a girl.

Seward: I know. Actually, I hear the old place has been sold. Goodness knows who would buy the old ruin.

Narrator 2: As Dr. Seward talks, Mina notices a strange man quietly entering the room. He's very large and strong, with wild eyes. He is chuckling to himself. Soon, Seward turns and sees him.

Seward: Mr. Renfield, you know better than to come in here! *(to Mina)* I apologize for this intrusion. This is one of my patients, Mr. Renfield.

Narrator 1: Seward calls for a hospital attendant.

Attendant: Sorry, Doctor. I don't know how he got out of his room.

Narrator 2: As Seward and the attendant talk, Renfield creeps to the window and watches a fly as it perches on the sill. He snatches it and pops it into his mouth.

Seward: Mr. Renfield, stop that! You are not to eat any more creatures—not even flies or spiders.

Renfield: But they're really very tasty and nutritious, Doctor. They give me life. I know things that you don't know. I can feed ten flies to a spider, then when I eat the spider, it gives me such power. It's eleven lives all in one!

Narrator 1: The attendant drags Renfield back to his room.

Scene 5

Narrator 2: A few days later, the newspaper in Whitby reports an event that has the whole town buzzing.

Newspaper Article:

GHOST SHIP RUNS AGROUND

During last night's storm, a mysterious ship from the east crash-landed on the shore. A dead man tied to the ship's wheel was the only human found aboard. **Witnesses** say that as soon as the ship ran aground, an enormous dog emerged from the ship's hold, and bolted off into the night. The ship's only cargo is 50 large wooden boxes of dirt, labeled for delivery to the Carfax estate. . . .

Narrator 1: No one in Whitby suspects that the ship's dog is Count Dracula himself. Later that day, Dr. Seward writes in his journal.

Seward's Journal: I'm worried about Mina. Her maid tells me that last night during the storm, she was found sleepwalking. She was headed for the window with her arms stretched out. People act strangely during a storm. Mr. Renfield was very odd last night, too. He burst into my room, chanting, "He's here, the master is here!" Could it have anything to do with the mysterious ghost ship?

 Stop here for the Strategy Break.

Strategy Break

The following chart lists clues that foreshadow what might happen next. Beside each clue, write what you predict might happen later in the play.

Foreshadowing	What I Predict Might Happen
1. "You used to think that Carfax, the estate next door, was haunted."	
2. "I can feed ten flies to a spider, then when I eat the spider, it gives me such power. It's eleven lives all in one!"	
4. As soon as the ship ran aground, an enormous dog emerged from the ship's hold, and bolted off into the night.	
5. I'm worried about Mina. . . . She was headed for the window with her arms stretched out.	
6. "He's here, the master is here!" Could it have anything to do with the mysterious ghost ship?	

As you read the rest of the play, underline other examples of foreshadowing. Use them to predict what might happen next.

Go on reading to see what happens.

Scene 6

Narrator 2: A month later, the maid finds Mina in her bed, very sick. Dr. Seward examines Mina and writes his findings in his journal.

Seward's Journal: The patient is very pale and weak. She looks like she has lost a lot of blood. But where did it go? The only marks on her body are two tiny holes, like pinpricks, on her neck.

Narrator 1: Over the next few days, Mina becomes even sicker.

Seward's Journal: I have sent for my mentor from medical school, Professor Van Helsing of Amsterdam.

Narrator 2: Van Helsing arrives and examines Mina. Then he calls Dr. Seward into the next room.

Van Helsing: You were right to call me. I know exactly what troubles the young woman.

Seward: What a relief! What is it?

Van Helsing: She is the victim of a vampire.

Seward: A vampire? Are you insane? With all due respect, Professor, there must be some other explanation. Vampires don't exist!

Van Helsing: Young man, there are many things on this earth that exist without our knowledge. You must find a way to open your mind to the possibility of this vampire, or Mina will die.

Seward: I will if I can. What kind of creatures are you talking about?

Van Helsing: Vampires are persons who exist somewhere between life and death. They have been robbed of their souls. The only way they can remain on this earth is to drink the blood of innocent people, through two tiny holes in the victim's throat.

Seward: Mina has two little red marks on her neck!

Van Helsing: Worse still, vampires' victims do not merely die. They themselves become vampires, and must spend **eternity** drinking the blood of others.

Seward: But how could this happen to Mina behind our backs?

Van Helsing: Vampires can do almost anything to accomplish their goal. They can turn themselves into bats or wolves or dogs. They can **hypnotize**

their victims and control their minds, beckoning them in their sleep. It's possible that Mina herself doesn't even know it's happening to her.

Seward: How can we stop this villain?

Van Helsing: Vampires sleep in the ground during the day, and only wake to do their evil deeds once the sun goes down. So we only need to worry about Mina during the night. I know of several things that will protect her from the vampire, such as garlic flowers.

Seward: But we can't protect her forever.

Van Helsing: Quite right. We must kill the vampire. There's only one way to do it: We must drive a wooden **stake** through his heart. Only then will he rest.

Seward: If his victims become vampires, does that mean that Mina is now a vampire?

Van Helsing: No, as long as she is still alive, she won't become a vampire. But if he takes too much of her blood and her body dies, her soul will depart, and then all is lost.

Scene 7

Van Helsing's Journal: Tonight we lined the windows and doors of Mina's room with foul-smelling garlic blossoms. Then I constructed a wreath of them for the girl to wear around her neck. This should keep her safe for the night.

Narrator 1: But a few hours later, when the doctors come to check on Mina, they find a maid putting all the flowers outside in the hall.

Maid: When I checked on my mistress, I saw a huge bat pounding against the window. He scared me. I thought maybe he was attracted to the flowers, so I threw them away.

Van Helsing: Dr. Seward, brace yourself for anything we may find in there!

Narrator 2: They burst through the door to find Mina lying in her bed with a tall, thin old man bending over her. When he lifts his head, blood trickles down his chin.

Dracula: Good evening, gentlemen. My name is Dracula. I'll forgive this one **intrusion,** but let me warn you. Do not try again to fool me with garlic flowers. You are no match for the powers of Dracula. I have come to this country because my own land is too empty of souls. Yours is deliciously full of people, and I intend to stay and make them mine.

Seward: Old man, leave that woman alone!

Dracula: Silence, fool! You try my patience. I am talking about issues too large for your tiny mind to grasp. Trifle me no more.

Seward's Journal: What happened next was so fast, I almost didn't see it. Dracula flew at Professor Van Helsing like a giant bird. But at the last moment, Van Helsing produced a gold **crucifix** and held it in front of him. This seemed to scare the vampire, who evaporated into a mist, and floated out of the room through a crack under the door.

Scene 8

Narrator 1: Van Helsing and Seward revive Mina, but others are not so lucky. The next morning, an old couple down the road are found dead, drained of all of their blood. Professor Van Helsing realizes that if he doesn't find the vampire, all of Whitby could be in danger.

Narrator 2: Late the next afternoon, Seward and Van Helsing are talking in Seward's den when the attendant knocks on the door.

Attendant: Sorry to disturb you, Dr. Seward, but there is a man here to see you. He says his name is Jonathan Harker, and that he is Miss Murray's fiancée.

Narrator 1: Doctor Seward and Professor Van Helsing meet Harker in the hallway. He is very thin and pale.

Harker: Sirs, I have been on a terrible journey to a place of unimaginable horror. Somehow I managed to escape with my life and have returned to look for my fiancée. I am told that she is ill. What is wrong with her?

Van Helsing: You would not believe us if we told you. But let me ask you: Does the name Dracula mean anything to you?

Narrator 2: A look of terror crosses Harker's face, and he faints. A few minutes later, they are able to revive him.

Harker: I know Count Dracula very well. He is a vampire from Transylvania. And he's just bought the Carfax estate!

Narrator 1: Thirty minutes later, as the sun sets, Seward, Van Helsing, and Harker head cautiously down the cellar stairs of the Carfax estate. As they reach the bottom, they see a large, coffin-like box in the middle of the floor.

Harker: That's it. Be very careful. He's very clever.

Narrator 2: They open the lid of Dracula's coffin.

Van Helsing: There lies the monster, neither alive nor dead. The fresh blood of the innocent Mina is still on his hideous lips. Time is of the essence. Hand me the wooden stake and the mallet.

Renfield: Not so fast, Doctor!

Narrator 1: The mental patient, Renfield, stands in the shadows with a pistol aimed at the men.

Seward: Renfield! What are you doing here?

Renfield: The Master knew you would come. He summoned me to protect him.

Seward: So that's what all your antics have been about. Dracula is controlling your mind. Don't you understand? He's evil! He'll destroy your soul!

Renfield: The sunlight will be all gone in a few minutes. Then the Master will rise and you can discuss it with him.

Van Helsing (whispering): He's right. This is our only chance.

Narrator 2: Harker tackles Renfield and takes his gun. At that moment, Dracula begins to stir.

Harker: Do it now, Professor, while he is still weak from sleep.

Narrator 1: Van Helsing pounds the stake into Dracula's heart. A terrible scream comes from the monster's lips, as bloody foam forms around them. Moments later, Dracula's entire body turns to sand, and disappears.

Van Helsing: It is over, gentlemen. The curse is lifted.

Narrator 2: They all return to check on Mina.

Seward: She's barely awake. But she looks better already, and the wounds are gone from her neck.

Mina: Jonathan, is that you? You're alive!

Harker: It's all over, Mina. We're together, and we're free! ●

Strategy Follow-up

Look back at the examples of foreshadowing that you underlined. Now that you know the ending, do you see even more examples? Get together with a partner or a small group to share the passages that you underlined.

✓ Personal Checklist

Read each question and put a check (✓) in the correct box.

1. How well do you understand what vampires are supposed to be?
   - ☐ 3 (extremely well)
   - ☐ 2 (fairly well)
   - ☐ 1 (not well)

2. In the Vocabulary Builder, how many words did you correctly match with their synonyms?
   - ☐ 3 (6–7 words)
   - ☐ 2 (3–5 words)
   - ☐ 1 (0–2 words)

3. How well do you understand what happens to Mina in this play?
   - ☐ 3 (extremely well)
   - ☐ 2 (fairly well)
   - ☐ 1 (not well)

4. How well do you understand why Harker says that he and Mina are free at the end of the play?
   - ☐ 3 (extremely well)
   - ☐ 2 (fairly well)
   - ☐ 1 (not well)

5. How well were you able to use foreshadowing to predict what might happen next in this play?
   - ☐ 3 (extremely well)
   - ☐ 2 (fairly well)
   - ☐ 1 (not well)

Vocabulary Check

Look back at the work you did in the Vocabulary Builder. Then answer each question by circling the correct letter.

1. Which word is a synonym for *eternity*?
   a. forever
   b. never
   c. ending

2. Which word might describe a haunted castle?
   a. closed
   b. dusty
   c. spooky

3. Which word means the same as *intrusion*?
   a. invasion
   b. separation
   c. reunion

4. Which word means "observer"?
   a. stake
   b. witness
   c. hypnotize

5. What letter does a crucifix look most like?
   a. an *X*
   b. a *T*
   c. a *Z*

Add the numbers that you just checked to get your Personal Checklist score. Fill in your score here. Then turn to page 205 and transfer your score onto Graph 1.	Personal		
	Vocabulary		
	Strategy		
	Comprehension		
	TOTAL SCORE		
		✓	T

Check your answers with your teacher. Give yourself 1 point for each correct answer, and fill in your Vocabulary score here. Then turn to page 205 and transfer your score onto Graph 1.	Personal		
	Vocabulary		
	Strategy		
	Comprehension		
	TOTAL SCORE		
		✓	T

Strategy Check

Review the examples of foreshadowing that you underlined in the play. Then answer these questions:

1. Which detail from the newspaper might have helped you predict that Dracula was in England?
   a. a storm causes a ship to run aground
   b. a dead man is tied to the ship's wheel
   c. a large dog emerges from the ship

2. Fifty large wooden boxes of dirt are labeled for delivery to the Carfax estate. Now that you've read the whole play, what do you think Dracula might have intended to do with the boxes?
   a. use them to store the bodies of the people he kills
   b. use the dirt to bury the bodies of the people he kills
   c. use the dirt to plant garlic flowers in his garden

3. At the beginning of Scene 6, if you had predicted that Dracula had gotten to Mina, what clue would have best supported your prediction?
   a. She looks like she has lost a lot of blood.
   b. She has two tiny holes on her neck.
   c. Both clues would have supported the prediction.

4. What does the line, "They can turn themselves into bats or wolves or dogs" foreshadow?
   a. Dracula will kill a bat, or wolf, or a dog.
   b. Dracula will turn into one of these creatures.
   c. Dracula will turn into sand and disappear.

5. Dr. Van Helsing tells Dr. Seward to brace himself for anything they may find in Mina's room. What would have been a logical prediction for what they might find?
   a. Dracula vanishing for good
   b. Dracula drinking Mina's blood
   c. Dracula driving a stake through Mina's heart

Comprehension Check

Review the selection if necessary. Then answer these questions:

1. Why is Mina worried at the beginning of Scene 4?
   a. Their wedding date is set, and Jonathan is going to miss it.
   b. It is not like Jonathan to be out of touch for so long.
   c. Mina thinks Jonathan is working way too hard.

2. Why do you think Mr. Renfield eats bugs?
   a. He is probably a vampire.
   b. The hospital doesn't feed him.
   c. He likes to scare Mina.

3. Why do you think Mina keeps getting sicker?
   a. She can't sleep at night because Dracula keeps scaring her.
   b. Dracula keeps visiting her and taking more of her blood.
   c. She can't sleep at night because she misses Jonathan.

4. Why was there a huge bat pounding against Mina's window?
   a. It was trying to get to the garlic flowers.
   b. It was Dracula trying to get to the maid.
   c. It was Dracula trying to get to Mina.

5. According to Dr. Van Helsing, what is the one way to kill a vampire?
   a. Put a stake through the vampire's heart.
   b. Hold a crucifix out to the vampire.
   c. Show the vampire a mirror.

Check your answers with your teacher. Give yourself 1 point for each correct answer, and fill in your Strategy score here. Then turn to page 205 and transfer your score onto Graph 1.	Personal	
	Vocabulary	
	Strategy	
	Comprehension	
	TOTAL SCORE	✓ T

Check your answers with your teacher. Give yourself 1 point for each correct answer, and fill in your Comprehension score here. Then turn to page 205 and transfer your score onto Graph 1.	Personal	
	Vocabulary	
	Strategy	
	Comprehension	
	TOTAL SCORE	✓ T

Extending

Choose one or more of these activities:

WRITE A NEW DIARY OR JOURNAL ENTRY

The diary and journal entries are an important part of this play. Choose one of the characters (Harker, Mina, Seward, or Van Helsing), and write what that character might have written on the day after Dracula vanishes.

CASTING CHARACTERS

Think about the characters of Dracula, Harker, Mina, and Renfield. What is unique about each character? With a partner or small group, brainstorm a list of the personality traits and physical features that someone playing each of these character should have. Then use your lists to write descriptions that you would use to advertise for actors to play these parts.

LEARN ABOUT VAMPIRE BATS

Vampire bats really do exist! But do they really suck other creatures' blood? Learn more about vampire bats by using one of the resources listed on this page. Or use sources that you find yourself. Present your findings in an oral or written report. Try to include pictures in your report too.

Resources

Books

Dracula Doesn't Drink by Debbie Dadey. Copyright © 1995 by Scholastic, Inc.

Movie Monsters by Thomas G. Aylesworth. Copyright © 1975 by J. B. Lippincott Company.

The Secret Life of Laszlo, Count Dracula by Roderick Anscombe. Copyright © 1994 by Hyperion Books.

Web Sites

http://www.birminghamzoo.com/ao/mammal/vampireb.htm
See a picture of a vampire bat and learn about where it lives, what it eats, and other interesting information—including how much blood it needs every day to stay alive.

http://www.jaguarpaw.com/Bats.html
This site will give you pictures as well as information about bats.

http://www.seaworld.org/animal_bytes/vampire_batab.html
Read some fun facts about vampire bats.

Learning New Words

VOCABULARY

From Lesson 11
• readjusting

Prefixes

A prefix is a word part that is added to the beginning of a root word. (*Pre-* means "before.") When you add a prefix, you often change the root word's meaning and function. For example, the prefix *un-* means "not," so adding *un-* to the root word *tied* changes *tied* to its antonym, *untied*.

re-

The prefix *re-* means "do over" or "do again." In Lesson 12 you learned that if you wanted to *readjust* your sleep habits, you would have to adjust them again.

  Write the definition for each word below.

1. reappear   _____

2. rebuild   _____

3. rediscover   _____

4. redraw   _____

5. reunite   _____

From Lesson 14
• transforms

trans-

The prefix *trans-* can mean "across," "over", or "through." In Lessons 14 and 15 Dracula transforms himself into a wolf, a bat, and a dog. *Transform* means "change over to another form."

  Complete each sentence with one of the words below.

transcontinental   translator   transparent   transfused

1. When a person's blood is removed and passed over to someone else, it is being _____.

2. A plane that travels across a continent is making a _____ flight.

3. When you can easily see through a window, that window is _____.

4. A _____ is a person who changes a person's words into another language.

Compound Words

A compound word is made up of two words put together. For example, in "Dava's Talent" the sheep are kept in a sheepcote. A *cote* is a shelter or shed in which animals are kept. So a *sheepcote* is a shelter or shed for keeping sheep.

Fill in each blank with a compound word by combining a word from Row 1 with a word from Row 2.

Row 1:   rain   road   tooth   week

Row 2:   runner   end   bow   ache

1. mouth pain caused by a cavity = _____

2. arch of colorful light = _____

3. speedy desert bird = _____

4. Saturday and Sunday = _____

Multiple-Meaning Words

You know that a single word can have more than one meaning. To figure out which meaning an author is using, you have to use context. Context is the information surrounding a word or situation that helps you understand it.

Use context to figure out the correct meaning of each underlined word. Circle the letter of the correct meaning.

1. I have an important homework assignment that I need to <u>tackle</u> this weekend.
    a. take on or deal with
    b. knock down

2. Harry is in <u>training</u> to become the store's new manager.
    a. making fit for a sport
    b. teaching a skill

3. These new glasses have really improved my <u>vision</u>.
    a. thing seen in the mind
    b. ability to see

VOCABULARY

From Lesson 11
- sheepcote

From Lesson 12
- catnaps

Lesson 13
- keepsakes
- whirlwind

From Lesson 13
- tackle
- train

From Lesson 14
- vision

When Disaster Strikes . . .

Building Background

If water were overflowing a river near your home, how would you stop it? One way people try to stop floodwaters is by sandbagging. A sandbag is made by taking a bag made of burlap or some other strong material and filling it with sand. The bag is then sealed and stacked to make a wall—or dike—which changes the flow of water. When communities are forced to sandbag, many volunteers work together. They make an assembly line in which some people make the bags, some people pass the bags, and some people stack them to build the dike.

copilot

life jackets

rope ladder

navigated

submerged

controls

hovered

Vocabulary Builder

1. Before you read this story, read the vocabulary words in the margin. Then talk with a partner about what might happen during a helicopter rescue. Use as many of the vocabulary words as possible in your discussion. If you don't know what any of the words mean, find them in context or look them up in a dictionary.

2. Sketch pictures or takes notes on your discussion. You will use your ideas again in the Vocabulary Check.

Strategy Builder

Using Foreshadowing to Make Predictions

- In Part 2 of *Dracula* you looked for examples of foreshadowing, and you used them to **predict** what would happen in the play. In this lesson, you will use foreshadowing to predict what might happen in "When Disaster Strikes . . ."

- Remember that **foreshadowing** is when an author drops clues about what might happen later in the story.

- As you read "When Disaster Strikes . . ." you will stop twice to make predictions. At each Strategy Break, you will write down which clues helped you make your predictions. Then, after you finish reading the story, you will look back at your predictions and check your work.

When Disaster Strikes . . .

by Cindy Trebus

As you read, look for examples of foreshadowing. They will help you predict what might happen next.

Stacey brushed the sand off her navy blue T-shirt revealing the words, I SURVIVED THE FLOOD OF SUMMER '93. She grabbed another bag for her dad to fill with sand and glanced toward the backyard. It was completely under water now. It's a good thing they'd decided to help sandbag, she thought. She could go for a ride in her dad's helicopter anytime.

"I'm afraid that's it for my back." Stacey's dad straightened up and groaned as a radio blared in the background. "Let's rest and let that busload of people do some sandbagging."

"We interrupt this broadcast to bring you a special news bulletin. The Meramec River is rising a foot an hour. Sandbaggers are desperately needed at . . ."

"I thought the water was rising fast," Stacey exclaimed. "Dad, why don't we go over to the airport and take the helicopter for a ride along the Meramec? That way we can check for people and animals that might be trapped by the rising waters."

Forty minutes later Stacey found herself sitting in the **copilot**'s seat. "Remember. Half an hour. That's it," her dad shouted. Stacey shook her head in agreement. She disliked trying to talk above the noise of the helicopter.

"Wait!" Stacey jumped out of the helicopter and ran into a nearby shed. After scrambling back into the cockpit, she held up two **life jackets** and a **rope ladder.** "Just in case," she yelled.

 Stop here for Strategy Break #1.

Strategy Break #1

Use the information in the story to help you answer these questions:

1. What do you predict will happen next?

_____

_____

2. Why do you think so?

_____

_____

3. What clues from the story helped you make your prediction(s)?

_____

_____

 Go on reading to see what happens.

Stacey gazed at the churning waters from the helicopter. Just imagine all those flooded towns, homes, schools, and trailer parks. She had hoped to practice flying her dad's helicopter more this summer, but they'd been busy sandbagging and helping people move. Now summer was almost over. Hey! What was that up ahead?

"I'm turning around. It's been half an hour, and I haven't seen anything," her dad said.

"Let's keep going. I see something over there," Stacey shouted.

Her dad leaned forward. "That's a roof sticking up out of the water."

"I see something on the roof," Stacey hollered. Her dad shrugged and **navigated** the helicopter toward the **submerged** roof. "I see dots. Three dots. And they're moving! It's three people, Dad!"

"What are they doing out here? They should've already left this area!" Grabbing the radio's microphone, her dad said, "This is 2360 Q. Our helicopter is about 10 miles south of Weiss Airport. We've spotted three people on a rooftop surrounded by the Meramec. The river is rising a foot an hour. Emergency equipment needed immediately."

"Where on the Meramec are you?" a voice crackled over the radio.

"Between the Arnold and Telegraph bridges where the Meramec divides St. Louis County and Jefferson County."

"The closest helicopter is 45 minutes away. Do you have the equipment and manpower necessary for a rescue attempt?" the voice asked, anxiously.

After a brief pause, her dad said, "Yes. There are two of us and a rope ladder, but we'll need specific directions. We've never done this before."

Stacey turned away and stared at the river. Just a few days ago four people were rescued by the State Water Patrol after hanging onto tree branches for eight hours. Six people had died in Cliff Cave due to flash flooding. Four of them were kids her age. The cave was 10 minutes away from her house!

It all seemed like a horrible nightmare, but it wasn't. Now she was in a helicopter above the Meramec watching helplessly as the river threatened to claim three more lives.

"Stacey, here's the plan. I'm going to circle the helicopter above them. When I'm ready, come here and take the **controls**," her dad said.

"But, Dad, I've only flown . . ." Stacey began.

"Stacey, you can do this. You know where the controls are and what they do. I have to attach the rope ladder to the cargo tiedown rings in the back."

As the helicopter began to circle above the three dots on the river, Stacey closed her eyes. She felt as if she'd gotten on a roller coaster ride too soon after eating. Her stomach was queasy, and her palms were sweaty.

Stop here for Strategy Break #2.

Strategy Break #2

Use the information in the story to help you answer these questions:

1. Do your earlier predictions match what happened? _____ Why or why not?

_____

_____

2. What do you predict will happen next?

_____

_____

3. Why do you think so?

_____

_____

4. What clues from the story helped you make your prediction(s)?

_____

_____

➡ **Go on reading to see what happens.**

"Come take the controls, Stacey," her dad shouted.

Stacey licked her lips and tried to swallow. She took a couple of deep breaths and stood up. Even though her legs felt like Jell-O, she made it to the pilot's seat.

Her dad hurried to the back of the helicopter. After what seemed like a long time, he grabbed the life jackets and rushed back to his seat, unfolding the ladder as he went. "OK. The ladder's secure."

As the helicopter **hovered** directly above the people, Stacey found herself back in the copilot's seat putting on her life jacket. She kicked the door open and let the ladder fall toward them. She could see their faces now. The man and woman appeared to be old and tired. The girl looked as if she was younger than Stacey.

Stacey looked anxiously at her dad. "It doesn't reach. We need to get closer."

"Tell me when I'm close enough," her dad shouted.

Looking back over her shoulder, Stacey yelled, "Lower. There's a girl down there about my height. Lower. Just a little lower. Stop!"

First came the girl. Then the woman. Stacey helped the woman into the helicopter. She crawled over, sat down, and put her arms around the girl. The man slowly climbed up the ladder. Stacey peered down at his weary face. Just then the man slipped. Still holding on, he managed to regain his footing.

"There are only a few more rungs. Then I'll be able to help you. Can you make it?" Stacey shouted. The man nodded and continued climbing. "There. Nice and easy. That's it. I've got you!" She grabbed the man's hand and pulled him into the helicopter.

As they were getting ready to leave for Weiss Airport, a helicopter came into view. Stacey glanced down where the roof had been and gulped. Her dad put his hand on her shoulder. "It's a good thing you wanted to take a ride along the Meramec—not to mention thinking of bringing life jackets and a rope ladder!" ●

Strategy Follow-up

Go back and look at the predictions that you wrote in this lesson. Do any of them match what actually happened in the story? Why or why not?

_____

_____

_____

_____

_____

_____

_____

✓Personal Checklist

Read each question and put a check (✓) in the correct box.

1. How well do you understand why sandbagging is important during a flood?
   - ☐ 3 (extremely well)
   - ☐ 2 (fairly well)
   - ☐ 1 (not well)

2. How many vocabulary words were you and your partner able to use in your discussion about a helicopter rescue?
   - ☐ 3 (6–7 words)
   - ☐ 2 (3–5 words)
   - ☐ 1 (0–2 words)

3. How well were you able to use foreshadowing to predict what would happen next in this story?
   - ☐ 3 (extremely well)
   - ☐ 2 (fairly well)
   - ☐ 1 (not well)

4. How well do you understand why the people were on the roof of their house?
   - ☐ 3 (extremely well)
   - ☐ 2 (fairly well)
   - ☐ 1 (not well)

5. How well do you understand why the timing of the rescue was so important?
   - ☐ 3 (extremely well)
   - ☐ 2 (fairly well)
   - ☐ 1 (not well)

Vocabulary Check

Look back at the work you did in the Vocabulary Builder. Then answer each question by circling the correct letter.

1. Which phrase best defines the job of a copilot?
   a. flies the aircraft
   b. helps fly the aircraft
   c. rides in the aircraft

2. For what are life jackets used?
   a. to help people climb rope ladders
   b. to help people learn to swim
   c. to help people stay afloat in water

3. If you navigated a helicopter, what would you have done?
   a. steered the helicopter
   b. watched the helicopter
   c. landed the helicopter

4. The roof of a house is submerged in this story. What does *submerged* mean?
   a. The roof is covered with water.
   b. The roof is covered with sand.
   c. The roof is high in the air.

5. What would you say a helicopter was doing if it hovered over your house?
   a. It moved in a big circle.
   b. It hung in one place.
   c. It flew past your house.

Add the numbers that you just checked to get your Personal Checklist score. Fill in your score here. Then turn to page 205 and transfer your score onto Graph 1.

Personal	
Vocabulary	
Strategy	
Comprehension	
TOTAL SCORE	✓ T

Check your answers with your teacher. Give yourself 1 point for each correct answer, and fill in your Vocabulary score here. Then turn to page 205 and transfer your score onto Graph 1.

Personal	
Vocabulary	
Strategy	
Comprehension	
TOTAL SCORE	✓ T

Strategy Check

Look back at what you wrote at each Strategy Break. Then answer these questions:

1. At Strategy Break #1, if you predicted that Stacey and her dad would find someone, which clue would have helped?

   a. Stacey and her dad are filling sandbags.

   b. "I'm afraid that's it for my back."

   c. Stacey runs back for life jackets and a ladder.

2. What does the news bulletin that "the Meramec River is rising a foot an hour" suggest?

   a. Someone is likely to get caught in the river.

   b. The river will stop rising very soon.

   c. The volunteers can all go home soon.

3. Which clue best foreshadows the fact that Stacey and her dad will perform the rescue themselves?

   a. "Where on the Meramec are you?"

   b. "Between the Arnold and Telegraph bridges where the Meramec divides."

   c. "Do you have the equipment and manpower necessary for a rescue attempt?"

4. At Strategy Break #2, what would have been a likely prediction?

   a. Stacey will be afraid when she goes to fly.

   b. She will have no idea how to fly.

   c. She will decide to never fly again.

5. Why do you think the author might have written, "But, Dad, I've only flown . . ."?

   a. to suggest that Stacey has taken over the controls as the pilot

   b. to suggest that Stacey has never taken over the controls as the pilot

   c. to suggest that Stacey has never flown in a helicopter before

Comprehension Check

Review the story if necessary. Then answer these questions:

1. How does the special news bulletin about the rising waters affect Stacey?

   a. She doesn't care about it and would rather be having fun in the helicopter.

   b. She thinks about taking the helicopter out to try and find trapped people.

   c. She thinks about how much her back will hurt from all the sandbagging.

2. Which words best describe Stacey?

   a. thoughtful and brave

   b. selfish and lazy

   c. shy and afraid

3. Why don't Stacey and her dad wait for the rescue helicopter?

   a. Stacey and her dad are too interested in being heroes.

   b. The water will cover the house by the time the rescue team arrives.

   c. They've never rescued anyone before, and they want to try it.

4. How does the author increase suspense?

   a. She includes the fact that others have been killed by this flood.

   b. She includes the fact that Stacey has not had time to practice flying.

   c. Both of the above answers are correct.

5. Why does Stacey gulp when she looks down after the rescue helicopter arrives?

   a. She thinks that she and her dad might be in the rescuers' way.

   b. See sees that the roof of the house is now completely underwater.

   c. She wants to alert the rescue helicopter to the trouble below.

Check your answers with your teacher. Give yourself 1 point for each correct answer, and fill in your Strategy score here. Then turn to page 205 and transfer your score onto Graph 1.

	Personal	
	Vocabulary	
	Strategy	
	Comprehension	
	TOTAL SCORE	
	✓ T	

Check your answers with your teacher. Give yourself 1 point for each correct answer, and fill in your Comprehension score here. Then turn to page 205 and transfer your score onto Graph 1.

	Personal	
	Vocabulary	
	Strategy	
	Comprehension	
	TOTAL SCORE	
	✓ T	

Extending

Choose one or more of these activities:

LEARN ABOUT MAJOR FLOODS

Find out about some of our country's major floods by reading one or more of the books listed on this page. Use a map, and make a poster to show and describe where the damage was.

COMPARE FLOODS

Choose two or more rivers that have flooded in the past few years, either near your home or in one of the books listed on this page. Compare how fast and how high the waters rose. Also compare the damage done to property and the number of lives lost in each flood. Use a comparison chart to compare the results of each flood.

LEARN ABOUT DISASTER ASSISTANCE PROGRAMS

Find out about how the American Red Cross and the Salvation Army help out in a disaster. Interview someone who works for one of these nonprofit agencies, or write a letter to your local or regional office. Decide which questions to ask in advance. For example:

- Who calls you when there is a disaster?
- In what ways do you give help?
- Where do you get the food and money that you give to people in disasters?

Resources

Books

Flood by Paul Bennett. Copyright © 1999 by Smart Apple Media.

Floods by Paul Sipiera and Diane Sipiera. Copyright © 1998 by Children's Press.

The Great Midwest Flood of 1993 by Carole Vogel. Copyright © 1995 by Little, Brown & Company.

The Mighty Midwest Flood: Raging Rivers by Carmen Bredeson. Copyright © 1999 by Enslow Publishers, Inc.

Web Sites

http://www.umi.com/hp/Support/K12/GreatEvents/Flood.html
Read news reports of the Midwest Flood of 1993.

http://www.nwrfc.noaa.gov/floods/papers/ch–2/great.htm
Learn all about the flood of 1993, including the area it covered and the damage it did.

http://www.crh.noaa.gov/arx/93flood.html
Compare flood crests of the 1993 and the 1997 floods in Midwestern towns.

Seed Travel

Building Background

In this lesson you will read about how seeds travel. You know that seeds need sunlight, air, water, and food to grow. Talk with a group of classmates about why and how seeds might travel to find these things.

Vocabulary Builder

glide

hitchhike

launch

nourishes

parachutes

pods

species

whirls

1. Before you read "Seed Travel," read the vocabulary words in the margin. If you don't know what any of the words mean, find them in the selection and use context to figure them out.

2. If that doesn't help, discuss them with a classmate or look them up in a dictionary. Then match the vocabulary words in Column 1 to their definitions in Column 2.

3. Save your work. You will use it again in the Vocabulary Check.

COLUMN 1	COLUMN 2
glide	catch a ride with someone or something else
hitchhike	provides food for
launch	move smoothly and easily
nourishes	type or class
parachutes	shells or coverings around seeds
pods	send off or send forth
species	spins or twirls
whirls	things used to fall slowly through the air

Strategy Builder

Comparing and Contrasting While You Read

- Authors often compare and contrast things when they write. **Comparing** means telling how two or more things are alike. **Contrasting** means telling how two or more things are different.

- Read the following passage. It compares and contrasts some different kinds of flowers.

If you have a garden plot, think about growing these great flowers. A morning glory grows on a vine, so choose a sunny place where you can provide a fence or a trellis for it to climb. It blooms from summer through early fall with beautiful blue, pink, or white flowers.

Impatiens are the perfect choice for a shady garden or border. A variety of colors, including coral, orange, pink, red, and white will bloom all summer long! Just remember to pinch back the early buds to get full, bushy plants.

Another pretty flower is the sweet pea, which also grows on a vine. Plant it next to a fence in full sun, and watch the blue, pink, rose, and white flowers bloom from early spring to early summer.

The sunflower can also be an exciting addition to your flower garden. As its name suggests, this tall plant loves the sun. It blooms with a head full of seeds and leaves of yellow and red in the late summer.

- If you wanted to show how these flowers are alike and different, you could create a **features chart**. It would look something like this:

	needs a sunny area	has summer blooms	includes white blossoms	grows on a vine
morning glory	yes	yes	yes	yes
impatiens	no	yes	yes	no
sweet pea	yes	yes	yes	yes
sunflower	yes	yes	no	no

Seed Travel

by Ann Ackroyd

As you read this article, apply the strategies that you just learned. Notice how the author compares and contrasts the ways in which seeds travel.

We like to think only humans use rockets, helicopters, **parachutes**, and gliders, but that's not true. Other travelers used such methods long before we did. These travelers are seeds! But why would a seed need to travel?

Seeds need to get away from their parent plants. If they remain too close, young plants starve. Their bigger, stronger parents overshadow them, hogging sunlight and water. It's also a seed's job to claim new living space for its **species**.

Have you ever watched a toy rocket take off with a small explosion? The Mediterranean squirting cucumber behaves like a rocket—without the fire. The little cucumber fills with juice until it's so full, it bursts off its stalk. A trail of slime follows it as it shoots through the air. This slime contains the seeds.

Plants with **pods launch** their seeds using another kind of explosion. When broom seeds are ready, the sun warms one side of the pod and dries it. The other side remains in shadow and dries more slowly. The sides pull against each other until the pod splits, hurling the seeds away from the parent plant. A Brazilian tree called the monkey's dinner bell does the same. It pops so loudly, strangers think they are under attack. The seeds can travel 40 feet, so it's best not to be in the way.

Many seeds use parachutes. Think of dandelion puffs—they contain hundreds of tiny seeds, each with its own silky parachute for riding the wind. Milkweed seeds come in pods instead of blowballs. If you open a ripe milkweed pod, you will see a packaging miracle. Hundreds of seed heads overlap neatly, while their closed parachutes lie flat, resembling hair.

 Stop here for the Strategy Break.

Strategy Break

If you were to begin a features chart for the article so far, it might look like this:

	launches like a rocket	pod splits	uses parachutes
Mediterranean squirting cucumber	yes	no	no
broom	no	yes	no
monkey's dinner bell	no	yes	no
dandelion	no	no	yes
milkweed	no	no	yes

 Go on reading.

Some seeds have wings to help them **glide** away from their parent plants. The simplest designs have one wing. Have you ever seen pine seeds leave an open cone? If so, you know that each seed sits at the base of a paper-thin wing. As the seed falls, it **whirls** through the air like a helicopter blade. The seeds of the alsomitra, an Asian creeper, also have one wing, but instead of spinning like helicopter blades, they sail like gliders. This is because the seed sits in the middle of the wing.

The Asian anisoptera has seeds with two wings instead of one. They spin because one wing is shorter than the other. If you live near maples or sycamores, you might think their seeds have two wings. Actually, each seed has one wing, and the seeds grow in pairs.

Some seeds travel in water by floating. The coconut is one example. Air spaces between its outer shell and the hairy inner seed keep it from sinking. A sweet, milky liquid in the center **nourishes** the seed.

The sea bean provides its seeds with wooden cases that can stay afloat for a year. These seeds ride the Gulf Stream and sometimes land in Europe—4,000 miles away from their parents in the Caribbean.

Many seeds **hitchhike**. Some use hooks to grab an animal's fur or a person's clothing. The next time you pull cockleburs from your socks, remember that you are helping the burdock plant expand its territory.

Other hitchhiking seeds ride inside the animals that eat them. They do this by hiding in fruits like strawberries and raspberries. All such hitchhikers have the advantage of landing in a pile of fertilizer!

A number of plants use only one seed carrier. Oaks and hickories belong to this group. The armor around their seeds is so thick, only a squirrel can break it. However, a squirrel collects more acorns and hickory nuts than it can eat. It hides the extras to eat later. But the extras aren't always needed, and sometimes a squirrel forgets its hidden treasure. The uneaten seeds grow into new trees far from their parents.

Look around and see if you can find more seedy rockets, helicopters, parachutes, hitchhikers, and floaters. Or what about seeds that travel in other ways? Look at a poppy, for instance. It acts like a salt shaker, shaking out its seeds. Once you start noticing how seeds travel, you'll want to make your own list. ●

Strategy Break

Now fill in this features chart for the second part of "Seed Travel." Go back and skim the article for information when you need to.

	glides (by whirling, sailing, or spinning)	floats in water	hitchhikes	shakes
pine				
alsomitra				
Asian anisoptera				
maple				
sycamore				
coconut				
sea bean				
burdock				
oak				
hickory				
poppy				

✓Personal Checklist

Read each question and put a check (✓) in the correct box.

1. In Building Background, how well were you able to brainstorm why and how seeds travel?
   - ☐ 3 (extremely well)
   - ☐ 2 (fairly well)
   - ☐ 1 (not well)

2. In the Vocabulary Builder, how many words were you able to match with their definitions?
   - ☐ 3 (6–8 words)
   - ☐ 2 (3–5 words)
   - ☐ 1 (0–2 words)

3. How well do you understand the different ways in which seeds travel?
   - ☐ 3 (extremely well)
   - ☐ 2 (fairly well)
   - ☐ 1 (not well)

4. How well do you understand the reasons why seeds travel?
   - ☐ 3 (extremely well)
   - ☐ 2 (fairly well)
   - ☐ 1 (not well)

5. How well were you able to complete the features chart in the Strategy Follow-up?
   - ☐ 3 (extremely well)
   - ☐ 2 (fairly well)
   - ☐ 1 (not well)

Vocabulary Check

Look back at the work you did in the Vocabulary Builder. Then answer each question by circling the correct letter.

1. Which word is most related to how a plant gets food?
   - a. hitchhikes
   - b. nourishes
   - c. species

2. Which method of travel is most closely related to the word *launch*?
   - a. rocket
   - b. helicopter
   - c. airplane

3. What do you call the shells or coverings around seeds?
   - a. glides
   - b. pods
   - c. wings

4. Which word means "type or class"?
   - a. pods
   - b. parachutes
   - c. species

5. Which two words describe how seeds travel?
   - a. *species* and *whirls*
   - b. *nourishes* and *parachutes*
   - c. *glide* and *hitchhike*

Add the numbers that you just checked to get your Personal Checklist score. Fill in your score here. Then turn to page 205 and transfer your score onto Graph 1.

Personal	
Vocabulary	
Strategy	
Comprehension	
TOTAL SCORE	

✓ T

Check your answers with your teacher. Give yourself 1 point for each correct answer, and fill in your Vocabulary score here. Then turn to page 205 and transfer your score onto Graph 1.

Personal	
Vocabulary	
Strategy	
Comprehension	
TOTAL SCORE	

✓ T

Strategy Check

Review the features charts for both parts of this selection. Then use them answer these questions:

1. What do oak and hickory seeds have in common?
   a. They both glide by spinning.
   b. They both shake like salt shakers.
   c. They both hitchhike.

2. How are pine and burdock seeds different?
   a. pines travel by whirling, burdocks travel by shaking
   b. pines travel by whirling, burdocks travel by hitchhiking
   c. pines travel by hitchhiking, burdocks travel by floating

3. Which seeds get shaken out as if from a salt shaker?
   a. poppy seeds
   b. hickory seeds
   c. alsomitra seeds

4. Which seeds travel by using parachutes?
   a. broom and monkey's dinner bell
   b. dandelions and milkweeds
   c. oaks and hickories

5. How do coconut and sea bean seeds travel?
   a. by launching like a rocket
   b. by shaking
   c. by floating in water

Comprehension Check

Review the article if necessary. Then answer these questions:

1. Why do seeds need to travel?
   a. so they do not starve
   b. to get sunlight and water
   c. both of the above

2. When a seed travels, what is it doing for its species?
   a. providing new colors
   b. providing new spaces to live
   c. providing more food

3. Which tree has seeds that pop very loudly and travel 40 feet?
   a. the monkey's dinner bell
   b. the Mediterranean squirting cucumber
   c. the Asian anisoptera

4. Why is floating a good way for sea bean seeds to travel?
   a. The seeds are nourished by the water.
   b. They can travel up to 4,000 miles in the water.
   c. They can land right in piles of fertilizer.

5. What happens to the acorns and hickory nuts that squirrels hide but don't eat?
   a. They grow into new trees.
   b. They dry up and die.
   c. They grab onto animals' fur.

Check your answers with your teacher. Give yourself 1 point for each correct answer, and fill in your Strategy score here. Then turn to page 205 and transfer your score onto Graph 1.

Personal	
Vocabulary	
Strategy	
Comprehension	
TOTAL SCORE	
	✓ T

Check your answers with your teacher. Give yourself 1 point for each correct answer, and fill in your Comprehension score here. Then turn to page 205 and transfer your score onto Graph 1.

Personal	
Vocabulary	
Strategy	
Comprehension	
TOTAL SCORE	
	✓ T

Extending

Choose one or both of these activities:

LIST WAYS THAT YOU'VE SEEN SEEDS TRAVEL

Work alone or with a partner to create a list of other ways that seeds travel. Think back to your ideas in Building Background about *why* seeds travel to help you think of *how* they travel. Use some of the resources listed on this page if you need help getting started.

COMPARE AND CONTRAST SEEDS IN YOUR NEIGHBORHOOD

Work with the whole class or in a small group, and collect a variety of seeds from your neighborhood. Take some time to study and compare the seeds. Then create a features chart that compares and contrasts what the seeds look like and how they travel. (Don't forget to compare the seeds' insides too.)

Resources

Books

Ride the Wind: Airborne Journeys of Animals and Plants by Hinojosa. Copyright ©1997 by Harcourt Brace and Company.

Seeds: Pop, Stick, Glide by Patricia Lauber. Copyright © 1991 by Crown Books for Young Readers.

The Nature and Science of Seeds by Jane Burton and Kim Taylor. Copyright © 1999 by Gareth Stevens Incorporated.

Tiny Seedlings . . . Their Journey by June F. Esparaza. Copyright © 1998 by Thoughts in Motion.

Web Sites

http://www.chestnut-sw.com/seedhp.htm
Learn all about planting and starting seeds for your garden.

http://tqjunior.advanced.org/3715/seeds4.html
See cartoons about seeds, and learn some fast facts about seed travel.

Main
Idea

Main
Idea

Detail

Detail

Detail

Detail

Main
Idea

LESSON 18
Vegetables

Building Background

The selection you are about to read explains what vegetables are and how they are grown. Draw a concept map, or web, on a separate sheet of paper. In the center of the web, write the name of your favorite vegetable. In the surrounding ovals, write what you know about the vegetable, including how it looks, smells, tastes, and feels—and maybe even sounds.

As you read "Vegetables," find out what part of a plant your favorite vegetable is, how it is grown, and whether or not it is really a vegetable. When you finish reading, add to the web any new information that you learned about your vegetable.

fertilizers

fungicides

greenhouses

irrigation

pesticides

produce

truck farms

Vocabulary Builder

1. "Vegetables" uses several specialized vocabulary words. As you know, **specialized vocabulary** words are all related to a particular topic, such as basketball or figure skating.

2. Think about how the words in the margin might relate to vegetables. Then use the words to complete the word map below. (If you need help with any of the words, look them up in a dictionary.)

3. Save your work. You will use it again in the Vocabulary Check.

What are they called in grocery stores?

Where do they grow?

VEGETABLES

What helps them grow?

Strategy Builder

Summarizing Nonfiction

- Sometimes when you read **nonfiction**, you're given a lot of information all at once. To keep it straight—and to remember it better—it helps to stop once in a while to summarize. When you **summarize** a section of text, you list or retell in your own words the most important ideas.

- Think about how you might summarize these paragraphs:

When vegetables are harvested, some are sold to be eaten fresh, but a large part of the crop will be eaten later in the year. Fresh vegetables will eventually begin to rot, so they must be preserved in order to be eaten later.

Freezing is a widely used method of preserving vegetables. Freezing must be done very quickly so that the vegetables will remain fresh. Vegetables are cleaned and blanched, or boiled briefly, before they are frozen. Blanching preserves the taste of the vegetables and keeps nutrients from being lost. Frozen vegetables are the most nutritious type of preserved vegetables.

Drying is an ancient way of preserving food. It is also a good method of keeping in nutrition. Vegetables are washed and blanched before dried. Then they are placed in insulated cabinets, and hot air is blown over them until they are completely dry. Dried vegetables may be used in soup mixes or packaged meals.

Canning vegetables is another way of preserving them. Some nutrition is lost in the canning process, but canned vegetables are popular and convenient.

- Here is how one student summarized the paragraphs:

When vegetables are harvested, some are eaten fresh, but some will be eaten later. To keep them from rotting, the ones to be eaten later need to be preserved.

1. Freezing is one way of preserving. (Frozen vegetables are the most nutritious preserved vegetables.)

2. Drying is another way. (Dried vegetables are good for soup mixes and packaged meals.)

3. Canning is another way. (Some nutrition is lost in this process, but it's popular and convenient.)

Vegetables

by Susan Wake

As you read the first part of this selection, try to summarize the most important ideas.

What Is a Vegetable?

A vegetable is the part of a plant that we eat. It may be the root, stem, leaf, seeds, or even the flowers and buds of the plant. Some vegetables are eaten raw, others are cooked, and many can be eaten either way.

Some of the vegetables we eat grow wild, but most are specially raised. Some vegetables, such as potatoes, are easy to grow and are found in many countries. Others, such as yams, only grow in tropical climates. Certain vegetables, such as cabbages, thrive in cool conditions.

Vegetables can now be produced all over the world, even in places where they do not grow naturally. Plants that need warmth to thrive can be raised in enclosed buildings called **greenhouses**. **Irrigation** brings extra water to dry areas so crops can grow. Because of these and other farming methods, the vegetables in our stores may come from almost any part of the world.

 Stop here for the Strategy Break.

Strategy Break

If you summarized the first part of this selection, your summary might look like this:

What Is a Vegetable?

- A vegetable is the part of the plant that we eat. It could be the root, stem, leaf, seeds, flowers, or buds.
- Vegetables can be eaten raw or cooked.
- Some vegetables are easy to grow and are found in many countries.
- Others grow only in tropical climates or cool conditions.
- With greenhouses, irrigation, and other farming methods, vegetables can now be produced all over the world.

As you read the rest of this selection, keep thinking about how you might summarize each section.

